You
CW01432538
WONDER
VERSE
Cosmic Inspirations

First published in Great Britain in 2025 by:

Young Writers
Remus House
Coltsfoot Drive
Peterborough
PE2 9BF
Telephone: 01733 890066
Website: www.youngwriters.co.uk

Book Design by Ashley Janson

Softback ISBN 978-1-83685-845-4
Printed and bound in the UK by BookPrintingUK
Website: www.bookprintinguk.com
YB0654O

FOREWORD

WELCOME READER,

For Young Writers' latest competition *Wonderverse*, we asked primary school pupils to explore their creativity and write a poem on any topic that inspired them. They rose to the challenge magnificently with some going even further and writing stories too! The result is this fantastic collection of writing in a variety of styles.

Here at Young Writers our aim is to encourage creativity in children and to inspire a love of the written word, so it's great to get such an amazing response, with some absolutely fantastic pieces. This open theme of this competition allowed them to write freely about something they are interested in, which we know helps to engage kids and get them writing. Within these pages you'll find a variety of topics, from hopes, fears and dreams, to favourite things and worlds of imagination. The result is a collection of brilliant writing that showcases the creativity and writing ability of the next generation.

I'd like to congratulate all the young writers in this anthology, I hope this inspires them to continue with their creative writing.

CONTENTS

Independent Entrants

THE
CREATIVE
WRITING

Whispers Of A Shattered Soul

In the cradle of the night, where shadows weave
I dance with echoes and in silence, grieve
Moonlight spills like tears on the ground
A requiem for a spirit I never found

In the forest of forgotten trees
Where silver streams sing of fractured beams
I wander through the remnants of a whispered prayer
Mourning the laughter woven through the air

In the chambers of my heart, where shadows play
Each note reminding me of the price I pay
Like petals falling from the ancient trees
I gather the fragments searching for me

Come back to me, my forgotten light
In the tapestry of stars, we'll take flight
Hold me in the depths of twilight's sigh
For the soul I lost, how I try to keep alive

In the night's embrace, I will sing for you
A lullaby woven from dawn's soft hue
Though the shadows may linger and the heartache remain
I will dance through the shadows 'til I am whole again.

Ruby Wood (10)

Breaking The Salt Line

I dug through the sand, my heart pounding in my chest,
The shoreline oracle's words urging me on in my quest.
"When tides forget their ancient song,
The salt will know where you belong."

Suddenly, I felt
A hard, leathery surface
Brushing my fingers.

I pulled it out gently,
And it seemed like the seagulls were singing sweetly to me.
My fingers tingled with a growing unease,
And I gasped the loudest gasp in the seven seas.

For I recognised
The curly handwriting that
Lay in front of me.

The next few days were very strange -
As the sea began to shift and change.
I heard my mother's voice on the wind,
While sudden storms would thrash and spin.

The sea began to
Change, too - it opened a path
At the touch of me.

I walked through the crystal blue
My heart pounding in rhythm
It felt like I had walked a thousand miles -
Then out of the blue, a turret rose, with ancient, sea-worn tiles.

It was the Sea King's
Lair, feared by all villagers,
And full of silence.

I pressed ahead, now more curious than ever
Better to face him now than never.
I needed to know why fate had led me here -
To unravel the Sea King's secrets, dark and clear.

Soon, I was inside
Still tussling with his strong guards
And then - I saw him.
Each step he took came with a spin and a twirl,
His robe cascading with a thousand pearls.
But then I met his menacing eyes,
And feared he'd drag my buried lies into the skies.

"What brings you here, girl?"
He boomed with a voice like waves.
I slowly shrank back.

"Do you want a deal?" He pushed me more.
I remembered my mother writing of this before -
How she said yes and was never seen again.
So I shook my head and hid my pain.
"You should listen," he said.
"It won't result in death."
I still said nothing.
"Who was my mother?" I asked,
Trying to keep my voice unmasked.
His mouth curled in a cruel, cold twitch -
"Oh, she was just a dirty Salt-Witch."
I reeled in shock,
As though I'd fallen headfirst
Into a dark pit.
"And I killed her," he added with a sneer.
My heartbeat stopped. My mind turned clear.
I had been in line. I had her blood -
But now, I'd break the chain for good.
I knew what to do.
I would not follow her fate -
The end starts with me.

"With blood, I mark the end of the chain.
No salt-born spell shall leave me in pain.
I speak the words. I make the cut.
This curse is closed. This door is shut."
I pricked my finger
On a blade beside the throne,
Held it to my heart.
The Sea King gasped in pure dismay,
As ancient runes began to sway.
"That chant was lost ten years ago!"
He cried as he began to glow.
"Bye," I said softly,
As his glowing form faded -
And I turned and ran.
I fled back through the sea once more,
Far from the cries of those drowned before.
In the water, I trailed my hand,
Relieved, no Salt-Witch curse would stand.
At last, I could see
My own familiar shoreline -
Like it had waited.

Riyansh Yadav (10)

Anna's Mystery

Anna's fingers danced across the canvas, strokes of vibrant paint bringing her latest piece to life. She was lost in the world of art, where nothing else mattered but the colours and textures. As she stepped back to admire her work, her eyes landed on a book lying open on her desk. The words seemed to leap off the page, echoing in her mind: 'The truth is hidden in plain sight'. Suddenly, her studio door creaked open. Anna spun around, expecting her best friend, Emma, but instead, a stranger stood before her. Tall, with piercing green eyes, he handed her a small package. "For you," he said, his voice low and mysterious. "From an anonymous admirer."

As the stranger vanished, Anna's curiosity got the better of her. She unwrapped the package to find an antique book with a strange symbol etched onto the cover. The pages were yellowed and the words were written in a language she couldn't understand.

As she flipped through the pages, the symbol began to glow. Anna felt an eerie sensation, as if the book were alive. She tried to shake off the feeling, but her eyes kept drifting back to the words. Suddenly, the text transformed, revealing a hidden message: 'Meet me at the old library at midnight. Come alone'.

Anna's heart racing, she pondered the mysterious message. Who was behind this and what did they want? Despite her reservations, her curiosity propelled her toward the old library.

As she crept through the deserted streets, the symbol on the book seemed to pulse with an otherworldly energy. She pushed open the creaky door and a figure emerged from the shadows. It was the stranger from her studio, but this time, he wore a different expression - one of urgency.

"Anna, you're in danger," he whispered. "The book contains secrets that powerful people will kill to keep. You must find the artist who painted the symbol - the one who holds the key to unlocking the truth."

As he handed her a small map, the sound of footsteps echoed through the library. The stranger vanished into the darkness, leaving Anna alone and bewildered. With the map clutched in her hand, Anna felt a surge of determination. She would uncover the truth, no matter the cost.

But as she turned to leave, she noticed a phrase etched into the wall: 'The artist is not who you think'. Anna's mind reeled with questions. Who was the artist? And what secrets lay hidden in the symbol?

The adventure had just begun and Anna was ready to face whatever twists and turns lay ahead.

Violet Rigby (9)

The Pied Piper Poem

Down in Hamelin village,
By famous Hanover city,
Rats infested the place,
Oh it was such a pity.

"Rats!" the villagers screamed,
"They're following us everywhere.
Another day with them,
We shall not be able to bear.

They gnaw and bite and scratch and tear,
Every single item.
We wish we had a hero,
Who was brave enough to fight 'em."

Then someone came to Hamelin,
A brave man who was German.
He declared he would get rid of the rats,
And there would be no more vermin.

So many have tried, the villagers thought,
Would this really be the guy?
I guess we should give him a chance
If he really wants to try.

"I want that reward," the man said,
"It's destined to be mine.
I will save the village
And everything will be fine."

"Alright, alright," the mayor said,
"Just do the thing I ask.
You will get your payment
Once you do my task."

To do this he used a shiny flute,
It did just the trick,
Now he knew he made the right choice,
When choosing an item to pick.

The man began his music,
It echoed in the rats' ears.
Suddenly, the vermin followed the sound
And in the background was the rumble of cheers.

He took them to the river Weser,
There, they all drowned.
Now they're out of sight
And most likely shouldn't be found.

"Yippee!" they cried joyfully,
The rats have disappeared.
We don't know what we would've done,
If that man had not appeared.

"Ha, ha," the mayor laughed,
"Your pay we shall not give.
But thank you for helping us,
As the rats no longer live."

But wait, what is going on? they thought,
Is he taking the children too?
Oh no, oh no, oh no,
Whatever shall we do?

Why did we ever choose him,
From the very start.
All those poor children,
He's ripped this town apart.

So the rats are now gone,
But sadly the children are as well.
Quite a mixed-up story,
But a great one we shall tell.

For now this is the end,
But the story still goes on.
Whatever happened to the children
Were they forever gone?

Eva Akhtar (10)

Home

There is a place that I can go,
A place where everything is okay and I can see how my life should have been.
When my heart stops pounding and a mist that blankets my life lifts;
As easily as a thin fog.

I never thought there would come a time when I would have to lie to myself to be happy.
Where I would want to forget about my life, just for a few hours.
A few hours of silence, of peace.
Far beyond my reach.

It felt like all the lights had been switched off in my life,
And I was left in the darkness.
But I kept searching for the light;
Wandering in circles, again and again and again.

Lying to myself.
Telling myself I was okay.
I could feel the pieces of my shattered heart digging into my chest, but I just ignored it.
I hadn't realised how broken I was until somebody else did.

Because I hadn't been allowed to grieve.
Of everything, I hadn't been granted that.
I was trying to grieve somebody I barely remembered.
Because I had been too young when I realised the world wasn't all it said it was.

When I still believed in the tooth fairy, I was surrounded by death and destruction.
My walls were closing in around me and I was suffocating.
I felt like I couldn't breathe, and my chest was tight.
But I still believed that if I ate an apple seed, it would grow inside of me.

And now I am trying to remember a person who I only had for a few years of my life,
And they feel like a distant dream, wisps of a past life that I never really lived.
And I know that somebody who was once my whole world;
I now can't even remember.

All I have are photographs on a screen;
Small frozen scenes of a play I never remember acting in.
And I feel it is all my fault.
Because I want to remember.

But when I go to this place, my mind goes quiet.
Everything is still, and the voice in my head stops screaming.
My heart starts sewing itself back together, stitch by stitch.
And I feel maybe one day I might heal.

I can see the light.
Dim, but bright amongst the darkness that has surrounded me for too long.
A glimpse of hope, a shadow of happiness.
Enough to rekindle the fire in my soul.

Sophia Jacobs (11)

Eulogy Of The Thorned Bloom

Beneath the firmament's alabaster shroud,
Lay roses dead, sepulchral, proud.
Once blushed in carmine's opulent guise,
Now pallor and decay betroth their demise.

Petals, gossamer as a lover's whisper,
Shrivelled into parchment, brittle, crisper.
Fragrance an elegy that lingers faint,
An artist's phantom, a scented complaint.

Thorns, the sentinels, steadfast remain,
Etched in defiance, enduring pain.
Nature's diadems, jagged and stark,
Piercing memories in the umbral dark.

Dewdrops cradle their sepulchral throne,
Diamonds mourning a beauty flown.
Hues once rapturous in their bold serenade,
Muted now into shadows that never fade.

Yet, in their ruin, a harrowing lore,
A bloom ephemeral, yet destined for more.
For even in death, their whispers adorn,
A testament eternal - the rose and its thorn.

Khudeeja Begum (12)

Look Up And Wonder

Welcome to this enormous void,
An endless place sparking imagination and curiosity.
In an unrelenting deep space,
Many things are lurking in this infinite abyss.
Who knows what is yet to be discovered
Do you know what is found in this magical space?
Have you heard of the pink nebula and silky stardust paths?
The colourful comets leaving a neon trail of enchantment,
Just urging you to follow, but you just watch in awe.
Spectacular stars - balls of gas and helium,
Billions of giant lamps all at once,
Vibrantly glowing, lighting up our night sky,
Joining to form countless constellations.
Massive meteors dart through the sky,
Creating incredible illusions, you just need to witness
You won't believe that there lies other fascinating, faraway features
Astounding asteroids, magnificent clusters of rock and dust,
Carelessly crashing into planets like a ball through glass.
But who could forget the brilliant black holes!

Forging almighty cyclones of stars,
Blacker than blackout, darker than darkness,
Sucking in deep secrets, yet to be found
You might think that this is just space
Or an endless span of nothingness,
But when you get to know this awesome creation of enchantment and wonder,
When you witness some of the unimaginable sights of space,
When the stars beam down and fascination takes over your mind,
Then you will understand why
So look into our wonderful night sky,
And it won't be hard to spot something that will blow your mind.
Who knows,
You might be the one who discovers something new,
In this mind-blowing universe.

Theo Calafatis (11)

Greedy Pete

I looked after a baby pig
A little while ago,
But although he was so small
His appetite seemed to grow!

His owner was a farmer's wife,
The piglet had been so small
The other piglets pushed him out
And he didn't get any milk at all.

So, Mrs Johnson took him to the house
And fed him milk she'd warmed up
He drank it from a bottle
Then in a box of straw he was put.

When Mrs Johnson went on holiday
Pete had already become like a pet,
So that was why I looked after him
(She couldn't board him with the vet!)

On the first day that Pete came
I gave him veggie scraps to eat
Mrs Johnson said, "It's his favourite,"
And he saw it as a treat.

On the second day I had him
He slurped up gravy and mash
Then I gave Pete a bit of my sandwich
And he gobbled it up in a flash!

On the third day that Pete came to stay
I fed him a whole French stick.
Later on, he ate the cat's food
Which wouldn't have been my pick!

On the fourth day of Pete's holiday
He ate six hot cross buns
Then he munched through a tin of shortbread
And a cheesecake that was my mum's!

On the last day I looked after Pete
He wolfed down bananas and bread
Then three whole packs of biscuits
It was as though he'd never been fed!

That evening Mrs Johnson came
To pick up greedy Pete
She said, "Thanks for looking after him,
He looks like he's had lots to eat!"

Savannah Salisbury (11)

The Era Of Dreams: A Rainbow's Tale

In the wake of the storm, when the heavens weep,
A whisper of magic stirs from the deep.
With each drop that falls, a symphony hums,
Colours awaken; the universe thrums.
Golden sunlight fractures through teardrops of grey,
And the world shifts gently, as shadows give way.
An artist's brush strokes the sky with pure grace,
Painting bold arches in a vibrant embrace.
Crimson cascades into sunlit embrace,
Mellow oranges dance, igniting the space.
Soft yellows gleam brightly, like laughter set free,
Emeralds twinkle in euphoric glee.
Indigo whispers of depths unexplored,
While violet sighs of dreams yet adored.
A bridge from the earth to the vast azure sea,
A promise of hope, wild and free.
Each hue tells a story, a fragment, a song,
Of journeys and trials where brave hearts belong.
In the silence of beauty, in the calm after rain,
The rainbow reminds us: through chaos, there's gain.

So let us chase rainbows, with hearts open wide,
Embrace every colour, let our spirits collide.

For life's fleeting moments, like rainbows, must pass,
But they linger in memories, an eternal mosaic of glass.
In this arc of enchantment, where dreams intertwine,
Find solace in colours; let your spirit align.
For after the tempest, when the sun's golden glow,
Shows the magic of rainbows, our hearts come to
know.

Tonye Ebitonmor (11)

Bestie

When I go over to my bestie,
I know she's the only one who gets me.
From the gifts to the presents to the love and the joy,
I know she won't leave me for no boy.

Ooooh oh oh, you got me saying ooooh oh oh,
And I know, oh, oh you'll never ever go oh oh.
Woah oh oh, you got me saying woah oh oh,
Wherever I go, oh oh I know that you'll follow oh.

'Cause you're my bestie, Bestie,
Next to each other, we're on top.
Together we're always ready, ready,
We'll keep on going and we'll never stop.

'Cause you're my bestie, Bestie,
When I'm down, you go turn things around,
Whenever you're around, I never feel empty, empty.
You know you'll never catch me with a frown.

Together we always have our fun,
Hand in hand we always run.
You're someone I can lean on,
Our love shines as bright as the sun.

Ooooh oh oh, you got me saying ooooh oh oh,
And I know, oh oh you'll never ever go oh oh.
Woah oh oh, you got me saying woah oh oh,
Wherever I go, oh oh I know that you'll follow oh.

When I go over to my bestie,
I know she's the only one who gets me.
From the gifts to the presents to the love and the joy,
I know she won't leave me for no boy.

Emmanuella Ajayi (10)

Enjoy Little Things

In the big, grubby city of London, I live
Surprising nature abounds if you're willing to give
A moment to look past the grey concrete and grime
You'll see tiny wonders that blossom in time.

Grabbing my dog, we set off in the cold
Bounding, ears flapping, she's ever so bold.
It's crisp, my breath clouds but a ray warms my face.
I turn, my eyes closed, pausing in place.

Looking down, I see daisies, they reach high above
Through cracks in the pavement, they squeeze, push and shove.
Soft, springy moss in vibrant, bouncy, round clumps
Along walls, good for balancing, hopping and jumps

We enter the park, the vast sky hung with clouds.
My dog belts off, free, then seeks pats from the crowds.
I used not to reach the branch high up the tree
But now swing, dangle and giggle with glee

Next, we're detectives, we're hunting down feathers
From pigeon or peacock, they are all treasures.
I walk past a spot that everyone misses:
A hidden gnome village, one catching fishes.

We look for my friend, seeing if he is in.
We set up for chess - there's a prize if I win!

Back from our trip, the fresh air zinged my brain
It's time to relax..

... 'Til it's walkies again!

Beatrice Collier (9)

The Final Whistle

As the half-time blew,
The confidence inside me flew.
Sad and disappointed faces all around,
We all knew the champions were already crowned.
Our team was down two goals in the final of the biggest competition yet,
My dream is to get a goal in the back of the net.
Whether it was a header, a volley or stepping up for a pen,
It wasn't a case of if more of a case of when,
We all took a water bottle from the changing room pile,
I looked at my friend Megan trying to produce a smile,
Then came in Coach Jade,
We could do it, she believed in us,
We nodded our heads, we had to trust,
Maybe we could do this, maybe we could make a comeback,
All we had to do was give that ball a good whack,
We headed back onto the pitch ready to go,
Our newfound confidence was beginning to show,
After not one but two goals found for our team,
I thought maybe winning this competition was not a dream.

We had played 90 minutes with one minute of added time,
I knew it was my time to shine.
A corner was coming in, we were all set,
As the ball bounced off my head it spun straight into the back of the net.
3-2!
Before we knew it the final whistle had blown,
Roars and screams from the crowd,
I could not feel more proud!

Holly Bainbridge (11)

The Nostalgic Summer

BBQs with streamers, rust and speed,
Trading laughs for skinned-up knees.
Sprinklers spinning in the yard,
Hide-and-seek till lights came hard.
Sleep came with soft crickets' tune, windows open.
Back when time was soft and slow,
And every dusk had a golden glow.
BBQs with smoky skies,
Burgers flipped as fireflies rose.
Swimming till our fingers wrinkled.
Splashing under the sun and moon,
We'd dive in deep and float with ease,
Cool relief in 90-degree pools,
Toys drifted out of sight,
We stayed in the water till the night,
Popsicles that stained our lips,
Vanilla swirls and drippy drips.
Ice cream cones with chocolate tips,
Melting fast on fingertips.
We chased the truck when we learned that tune,
Each jingle like a perfect boom.
Sticky hands and rainbow sprinkles,
Cold bites gave us happy wrinkles.

The heat would shimmer off the street,
We'd fry an egg right on concrete.
Sweat would bead and slow us down,
But no one cared - we ruled the town!

Now those days are far behind,
But forever live in my mind
Summer breeze in each backyard,
Songs bring me back to where I belong.

Eiman Abdul (9)

Diving Into A Realm Of Symphonies

Diving into a realm of symphonies,
Indulging in the mystical path of harmonies,
One key makes the room twinkle like a celestial blast,
Every note echoing a unique sound - from the first to the last,
Melodies flooding back as the music dances around like invisible butterflies in the breeze.
Diving into a realm of symphonies,
Pouring in like a ray of sunshine on a rainy day,
Uplifting and joyous tunes drifting around,
Tunes soaring into the unknown,
Like a magical diamond maze.
Diving into the realm of symphonies,
Where the melodies sparkle amongst the harmonies like a shimmering star illuminating the night sky,
Bursting the colours in vivid, dynamic flames full of life,
And the crystal-clear pieces ripple like invisible fountains rolling down the slopes of music,
Among the mellifluous bubbles that cascade down the surface as the notes gently flood the room.

Diving into a realm of symphonies,
Like a hot air balloon rising into the haze,
Like cotton candy clouds gently floating in the breeze,
Like the trees swaying to the rhythm of the wind,
Like a heap of sparkling gems
Diving into a realm of symphonies,
Where music is the paradise...

Sameeksha Panigrahi (12)

The Tree Of Hope

I blossomed with life and I was oh so perfect,
My leaves fluttered with joy in the day and night breeze,
I stand tall reaching for the stars as I see other trees like me, some rising and some falling, hoping then resting peacefully,
And so, I thought, will I ever reach this peace?
As seasons changed and life went by,
I stood proud and still,
But one day a smell came up in the air, it was cruel, grey and was written with despair,
I tried to shake it off, but it grabbed on my leaves,
It slowly took control of it and it withered its bloodline and my beauty,
But that could not stop me as I stood on as just the normal tree,
The next day, it was my time,
As tiny figures cut and shaped and left me to die for someone else's use,
The light at the end of the cave closed as I was no longer the tree I used to be,
Then suddenly it reopened as I found... hope?

As I rested in heaven and my leaves fluttered again like never before,
I noticed I was not just a tree, I was the tree of hope and from the start, it was always inside me,
Whatever happens to me, good or bad, I will always stand proud even if I have fallen to the ground as the tree of hope.

Mrigaj Patel (11)

Growing Up Is Hard To Do!

Growing up is hard to do,
They say it's fun but that's not true!
I used to laugh and play all day,
But now I've got to sit and stay.

At school I try, I really do,
But it's got tougher, that is true.
They tell me to 'focus' when I stare outside,
But most of the day my brain's just fried.

Friends can be fun, we smile and play,
But sometimes mood swings get in the way.
Girls can be tricky but so kind-hearted,
And boys? Don't even get me started!

I have to try and be polite,
"Mind your manners, get it right!"
No using hands, "Oh, my life."
Now it's all fork and knife.

Growing up is such a bore,
Excuse me while I do a chore.
Now TV time is the worst,
I have to do my homework first!

Now I worry about what to wear,
How I look and "how's my hair?"
Do these clothes fit? Are they cool?
Will they work for after school?

Growing up is hard to do,
They say it's fun but that's not true.
I'm only ten, learnt a thing or two,
And growing up is hard to do!

Sophie Watkins (10)

Seasons

The seasons come and the seasons go
But where they go, I shall never know.

Spring, the prettiest by far,
Little blossoms drop to the ground
With not a sound.
The leaves blush with green,
Yet hardly seen.
Once in a while, a bird tweets,
But never as pretty as the petals, coloured like sweets.

Summer the next,
The sun high in the bright blue sky
As the wind gives a sigh.
Flowers open wide, embracing the heat,
Fragrant smells carried to the place where sheep bleat.
Every so often a butterfly lands
Straight on someone's hands.

Autumn comes too soon,
Those dry days are gone,
Rain drizzling on the lawn,
That bright green goes away
And so the reds and oranges sway.

The cold, creeping round the corner
To meet some sad mourner.

Winter, the harsh one,
Frost cutting, biting and snapping.
No mercy, it leaves you shivering,
Dancing snowflakes fall,
So beautiful and small.
As light as a feather
But this is still harsh weather.

So there you go, the never-ending cycle.

Zelene Tang (11)

The Mad Un-Inventor

Imagine a world,
That has been un-invented.
Think of all the problems,
That will be prevented!
No more boxing elephants,
To punch your nose!
No more crabs at the beach,
To pinch your toes!
No polluting pollution,
No smoking smokestacks,
No overcrowded,
Confusing bike racks.
No spots or pimples,
Or itchy rashes.
No tripping or falling
Or nasty crashes.
No waste, no rubbish,
No junk, no litter.
No texting, no Facebook,
No spamming, no Twitter.
No noise, no fuss,
No bother and mess.

No need to worry,
Or fret or stress.
No more noisy sporting events.
No more vacations in tiny tents!
No more warnings
About global warming.
No more boring
Boy bands forming!
No more fights,
No bites and bruises.
No more winners
And no more losers.
Nothing to lose!
Nothing to gain!
No more struggling!
No more pain!
How clean!
How pure!
How perfectly silent,
And how wonderfully peaceful,
Not at all violent!
Nobody could possibly,
Be disconnected,
In a world that
I have un-invented!

I'll get rid of the world!
I'll get rid of it all!
No more mistakes.
Not a single flaw!

Safa Patel (9)

The Orb Of Life

The world around me seems so still,
I look down to see myself sitting here,
Why am I not freaked out? But just curious instead,
I look in my hand to see an orb of light,
But why am I just sitting here, not doing anything?
I look at my clock... It's 10am,
What am I doing? I should be at school by now,
I have never seen that orb before, but somehow I know what it is,
It's the orb of life but why have I got it?
I'm not dead or am I?
Could I really be dead or is this a dream?
I pinch myself and I don't wake up,
It must be real,
But then I realise I didn't feel a pinch,
My hand goes through my body, I am just a cloud of smoke,
Hang on... is that my alarm clock I hear?
Everything goes black,
I wake up,
But what happened,
It can't have been a dream,
I crawl out of bed to find that same orb hidden under my drawers.

Lucie Toward (13)

Imagination Is Key

Imagine this -
You doodle a puppy in math class,
And *bam!* It jumps off the page,
It licks your face, eats your homework.
Your teacher yells, but you're not in trouble,
'Cause now her ruler's spaghetti.

The class gasps, then erupts in giggles,
As your best friend sketches a wiggle -
A marker-drawn shark with polka-dot flair,
Now chomping the chalkboard, thrashing mid-air.

The teacher sighs, but her frown can't stick -
Her coffee cup blooms a rose, thick and quick.
The bell rings, but no one moves an inch,
Too busy building castles from textbooks and lint.

You scribble a door on the locker room wall,
And suddenly, whoosh - it leads to a mall
Where the escalators are rainbow slides,
And the food court serves galaxy fries.

Reality's a story still half-told -
Your pen's not ink... it's starlight, pure and bold.
Your hand's a comet - scratch the sky's veneer,
And ink bleeds black holes where new worlds appear!

Andrei Ursut-Avram (11)

A Love Lost In The Abyss

I know that we are done, that's what I'm told.
All the words you said. Locked in my mind.
Error404: I'm left on a cliffhanger, falling into the abyss of broken promises that I worked so hard to escape from.
Letting our bridges burn, I gave you my devotion.
After all, only someone who once loved you can hate you the most.
And then you pushed me off the ledge, exactly how you slowly lost interest in me, slow but cold.
Now I wonder, awestruck in your behaviour. Was I nothing to you?

I believed we were meant to be. Although you simply mocked me, my love for you, the pain I endured for you.
Could this be a love never known to me?
How you treated me?
A love lost in the abyss, how could we ever go back to being friends?
Relinquished love, the war between my conscience.
Linked to my heart, you taught a lesson to me. One I had to learn.
I never thought you would truly make me love you, that's what I hate most.

Every fading morning, text lost in the depths of eternity.
Where our love withered like autumn leaves in the winter breeze.

Lily Kumbhat

The Ball Games

Bounce, bounce, bounce goes the ball around the pitch,
Carefully controlled by children.
Bounce, bounce, bounce goes the ball outside the box,
To be shot into the goal.
The goal has its mouth open wide,
Ready to receive the delicious ball.
The goal has its mouth open wide to swallow,
As the ball sails into it.
The goal spits it out again,
Ready for Round 2.
Bounce, bounce, bounce!

We've just had to leave (the game),
I've still got things up my sleeve (okay)
Thud, thud, thud,
Goes the ball in the mud.
Splash, splash, splash,
Lots of players get a bit rash.
The players want more,
The crowds start to roar.

Since we're playing by the sea,
Water crashes into me.
(Got an idea?)
We stop for a break,
Sandwiches, we need to take,
(Radishes are in there, I hate them.)
All of us here are gems,
This game will never end,
If we don't stop the beach volleyball game now.

Oluwaferanmi Adeyemo (11)

Who's That Girl?

Who's that girl over there
With scarlet eyes and ginger hair?

Who's that girl over there? Who is she?
Who's that girl over there, the one with blonde highlights and ginger hair?
Who's that girl over there? Who is she?
She is the one who is sitting by a tree,
Staring into space as if lonely,

With her eyes brown and shiny,
The girl who is always kind

She is the one with a gentle smile,
Gave the blackish brownish street cat her supper,
Her companion amazes everyone she meets,

She is the one who helped the elderly lady carry groceries,
But nobody saw her eyes like fire shine

For she is as beautiful as a lily in every single way,
So now nobody whispers, who is that girl?

She is happy.
She has a warm house and a cosy fireplace,

That was her favourite place where she used to cuddle
up and write poems...
Much like the one you are reading now, and that was
where she stayed for the end of her days.

Shanna Keshavarz Sarkar (9)

Portal In My Pencil Case

I opened up my pencil case,
And saw a glowing, spinning space.
It shimmered blue, it sparked with light,
Then zapped me up and took me on a flight!

I flew through clouds and zipped through stars,
On rainbow roads and candy cars.
The moon was shaped just like a pie,
And rocket whales zoomed past the sky.

I danced on planets made of cheese,
And skated down the milky seas.
A dragon waved and said, "Hop on!"
We zoomed around from dusk to dawn.

The trees were pink, the grass was teal,
I ate a cloud, my lunch was real!
The sun wore shades, the wind could sing,
And clocks were shaped like chicken wings.

But just as I began to cheer,
A voice rang out, "Math test is here!"
I blinked and dropped back in my seat,
With shaky hands and jelly feet.

Now every time I see that place...
That portal in my pencil case...
I smile wide and start to dream
Of magic lands and whipped cream streams.

Jamaima Zareen (9)

The Positive Person

The positive person is a nice guy,
He never says bad to people and never will say bye.

The way he talks is very nice,
He never uses poison or bad spice.

The positive person is nice and thoughtful,
He never thinks bad or is ever even doubtful.

If he were negative, what would it be like?
Well, he would be acting evil and breaking a bike.

But no, he never ever was like that,
He would not even ever swing a bat.

Yes he gets angry sometimes,
But he always changes his mood on time.

The positive person is never ever lying,
And he also never leaves anybody dying.

He is so positive the whole world stands up to him,
He is so rich he can also buy up to 5,600,000 dreams.

He would never speak bad at all,
But he talks so much his mouth moves as fast as a ball.

Soon enough, he will sadly leave,
But first, he will speak positively to himself as fast as a person can speak.

Mehaan Pathak (9)

Lunch On Olympus

I ate lunch on Olympus
Hermes stole a baguette
Aphrodite was a witness
The culprit wished she would forget

I had a sandwich with the gods
But Hades doesn't talk much
Poseidon started a conversation about fishing rods
Zeus complained that it was more of a brunch

I did a Sudoku with Athena
But Dionysus got me distracted
Chugging on an Orangina
This moment could not be reenacted

I had an ice cream with Apollo
But he got a brain freeze
Expecting the other gods to follow
Who were still munching on cheese

Unfortunately, I had to return to reality
So boring - it tests my sanity
Mere mortals offering biscuits and tea
"Where's your head at?" Mum sighed
"In Olympus," I replied.

My cat put her head to one side
Grandpa asked how the gods are these days
I said they were going through a bit of a phase
As I tucked into my second egg mayonnaise.

Iris James (11)

Cassie And Billie

There was a cloud called Cassie,
All fluffy and squishy.
She had a smile on her face,
As she watched down below.

She saw the trees blowing in the breeze,
And the flowers attracting bees.
Kids playing, laughing
And crying when they grazed their knees.

As she watched, she looked to the right
And there was Billie the birdie all alone.
She wanted to make friends,
But the only thing was
Billie was a bird, not a cloud.

They started talking.
They talked and they talked
And minutes turned into hours.
A new friendship was formed.

Days turned into weeks
And months into years.
As they got older, their friendship grew stronger.

Cassie and Billie were like family.
Even though one was a cloud
And one was a birdie.

They were different, but that didn't matter, because
Friendship gave them company,
Friendship stopped them from being lonely,
Friendship made them happy.

So be like Cassie and Billie
And make friends with everybody.

Sienna Kapur (8)

Mythical Mutters

"Help me! I'm drowning in chicks."
Lorenzo, the first-born chick, is afraid of the other chicks,
Even though they are younger.

All the humans hear is,
Cheep, cheep, cheep
But... humans can hear the other animals.
So animals have to be quiet
To keep their secrets kept.

"Helro! Hamanwy!"
Whoops, I shouldn't have said that"
"OOOrrro yurmumy! Little Checks!"
Bella the cat is like a panther,
Pouncing at anything she can find.

This time, the humans can understand,
So, if they listen closely to Bella,
They will hear a,
"Helro Hamanwy!"

"Hi, hi, hi, hi, hi, hi, hi, hi!"
Margot doesn't understand the magical, mythical gift of speaking,
So, she does a 'Hi' whenever she likes.

But what the humans say
Is rather unfair,
"Baddog!" Margot replies with a
"Haaarrrr!"

Harmony Tait (10)

I Wish...

When you're a child, you think that everything is possible; all your thoughts suddenly burst into life.

"I wish that I could fly,
I wish that I could fly high.
Over the treetops, over the mountains, over the clouds.
I could soar like an eagle; I could touch the sky.
I wish that I could fly."

"I wish to be a princess.
I wish to be a princess, to have fun that is endless.
In a palace warm, surrounded by diamonds, with lots of gold.
I could sit on a throne and not make any mess.
I wish to be a princess."

"I wish to have a unicorn.
I wish to have a unicorn with a very pretty horn.
Riding on rainbows, galloping through a forest, stroking its mane.
I could have so much fun eating popcorn.
I wish to have a unicorn."

"I wish to go to space.
To join in with the alien space race.
Looking at planets, dancing with the stars, dodging comets.
I could watch the stars, their dances full of grace
I wish to go to space."

Michelle Alenoghena (11)

The Adventures Of Nature

I'm soaring through the sky today,
The sky is so blue.
As I flap my wings,
There are so many beautiful things to do.

As I fly in the sky, twisting and turning,
Past the breeze.
I reach my first destination,
A bunch of tall trees.

I swoop into the trees to make a nest,
Then I sit down, curl up and rest.
In my dreams I think of life and
All the beautiful places I want to go.
I'd love to see the mountains,
Speckled with snow.

I wake up all bright and cheerful.
I've got this sudden rush of joy.
I'm soaring through the sky again and
I spot a pond with a little koi.

I've been flying for a week now
And my wings are getting tired.
But finally, what's that I see,
The mountains in the distance looking at me.

I do one last push,
Gliding past the trees of snowy slush.
I travel to the tippy top
And look at the amazing views.

I made it,
I made my dream come true.
I just love nature.
I really, really do!

Aaryan Kapur (10)

Wonder Girl

I wonder where I am now
This place makes me say wow
The trees are growing tall
I think it's nearly fall
I think I love this place
With butterflies to chase
I wonder where my parents are
I don't think they're very far
My parents are probably missing me
But I'm okay, if only they could see!
Maybe I miss my parents a bit
Sometimes I think and sit
I'm very lonely
I'm not being a phoney
I wonder how I'll get home
I miss the garden gnomes
I miss my cuddly bunny
She was very sunny
I miss all the hugs
And the hot chocolate mugs
I miss their warm kiss
Oh, how I miss, miss, miss!

I wonder if I'll see my dad
It is him! I'm very glad
I wonder if I'll see my mum too
I'm so happy! I do
I missed my mum and dad
They make me so glad
I wonder where I'll go the next day
Maybe I won't go, I'll stay.

Ivy Onuba (9)

Hope

Hope is a shining star,
Lighting up the darkest skies at night.
Hope is a glowing beacon,
Lighting up the way.
Hope is a shining lighthouse,
Helping lost boats find shelter.
Hope is a tiny seed,
Waiting to grow in spring.
Hope is a small baby,
Hoping to walk like her family.
Hope is a flickering fire,
Warming up people in Iceland.
Hope is a new book,
Waiting to be read by lovely children.
Hope is a victorious goal,
Lifting the scores up.
Hope is a bunch of colourful flowers,
Waiting to bloom.
Hope is a cuddly teddy bear,
Making children feel loved instead of worried.
Hope is a loving family,
Helping you along your journey.
Hope is a closed present,

Waiting to be opened and enjoyed by everyone.
Hope is God,
Protecting people from danger.
Hope is a big joke book,
Making hundreds of people laugh.
Hope is a colourful rainbow,
Making people smile.
Hope is our friends,
Sharing secrets.

Cosima McCabe (8)

Poem

O' South America
O' South America
Home of jaguars, spider monkeys, electric eel,
Red bellied piranhas, poison dart frogs leap,
Bull sharks and anacondas creep,
Capybaras wade in the river deep,
River otters play, hummingbirds sweep.
Harpy eagles soar so high,
O' South America under your sky.
O' South America so wild and free,
You have the most biodiversity!
O' South America
O' South America
You have the most species in the world.
The Amazon rainforest thrives,
With endless rivers and creatures inside.
A place of oxygen, life and wonder,
Thunder rolls, river runs under.
O' South America
O' South America
The Amazon is divided into four layers,
The forest floor, the understory,
The canopy and the emergent layer.

O' South America
O' South America
You are the richest land, life and colour!

Ibrahim Kashif (7)

Tell Me Leopard

Tell me leopard,
Are you happy walking around in circles
Trapped in your display case
Waiting patiently to be free?

Locked in despair
Your angry eyes
Your fiery heart losing flames
As you gaze into the skies

You should be roaming around freely
Snatching your prey
You want to leave but
The people make you stay

You're a nocturnal hunter
You should be slinking around
You're a silent hunter
Never making a sound

You should be strolling around proudly
Chasing around deer
Peering through long grass
Attacking your prey with no fear

But you're not, you're trapped behind metal bars
Locked in your concrete cage
Just you and your anger
Just stuck with your rage
Tell me leopard

Are you happy walking around in circles
Trapped in your display case
Waiting patiently to be free?

Jasmine Darrell Pearse (10)

Mother

Oh Mother, oh Mother, oh Mother.

My mom, you're a mom of loveliness,
My mom, when I see your eyes, I show my thoughtfulness,
My mom, you're a mom of loveliness.

My mom, you're so trustworthy,
My mom, you always encourage me to pursue my dreams,
My mom, you push me towards my goals,
My mom, you love me the most.

My mom, you sacrifice a lot for me,
My mom, you're so beautiful for me,
My mom, you're very kind,
My mom, you help me navigate life.

My mom, you're so funny,
My mom, I'm happy to be your bunny,
My mom, you make fantastic food,
My mom, you're always in a splendid mood.

My mom, you're so confident,
My mom, you're so hardworking,
My mom, you're all I need,
My mom, you being my mom is the most rewarding thing.

Oh my mom, I can't imagine life without you!

Omar Al-Jaberi (9)

My Head Teacher, My Hero

I was told not long ago
That people come and go
By someone very wise and not so old
That if you toss that one stone
Big ripples will start to unfold

I can say I had a great head teacher
Who helped me to grow
Inspired many young minds and was lovely to know
Someone who changed me and my world from the get-go
Never have I known someone
Through pain and suffering
To easily let go
Yet
You have helped shape young minds
To be able to explore all things big or small
It definitely takes that someone special
To kickstart that go
You taught us to strive, believe, be the best and never let go
I've seen you stop and stall
And still seen you giving it your all

I know one thing for sure
You will always be that someone who I will always adore
I'm glad Mrs Ttoffali, you were my head teacher
The best one I've ever known!

Gurmail Singh Ryan (9)

Animal Surprises

We are in the jungle as the sun rises,
A river wraps through the trees and delivers animal surprises!

Our first is furry and brown,
Playing and swinging from vine to vine,
Because he's a cheeky monkey,
Who is next in line?

Our sssecond is sssometimes ssscary and can have a dangerous bite,
It's a snake!
Did you get it right?

Our third lives in the river and has a big, toothy smile,
Have you guessed it yet?
That's right, it's a happy crocodile!

Our fourth has bright coloured feathers that you can see from far away,
Of course, it's a parrot!
It squawks and flies away

Our last sings and croaks to its friends,
Looking for insects to eat,
I am talking to a frog,
Today, that's the last animal we will meet,

We are in the jungle, the sun setting and changing to stars above,
I can't wait to visit again and meet more of the animals I love.

Tara Scott (8)

Tropical Thailand

Long hours sitting
Waiting and wishing
Soon to be there
Flying in the air

Busy Bangkok streets, lined with markets
Everything to buy from cakes to carpets
Looking at the palace, standing in awe
What we see through the golden door

Exploring Chiang Mai, food everywhere
Walking around, delicious smells in the air
What food to try, so much to see
My favourite, Bao buns, all for me

In the jeep, going up the hill
Sitting on the seat, feeling ill
Cross the mountain, climb up high
Look what's coming, elephants walking by

Koh Samui, final destination
Can't wait for rest and relaxation
Deep blue pool, by the sea
All for you and me

Bumpy boat ride, across the sea
In the damp seats, just you and me
Snorkelling around, looking for fish
Seeing a star, making a wish.

Alice Barrow (9)

The Great War

The dirty trenches filled with blood,
The whole thing fully caked in mud,
Just a taste of the suffering and pain,
That we endure again and again,
So I cannot wait for the bullet that belongs to me,
Or the shell that comes to set me free,
From this war, this tragedy.

11th November 11 o'clock,
We are all waiting for the fighting to stop,
The guns are still firing as this war blazes on,
I think of my friends, the dead and the gone,
Then suddenly, everything is silent,
There is no more fighting, there is no more riot,
The birds start chirping singing their song,
It is all over; the fighting has gone.

On no-man's-land the poppies grow,
Between the crosses row on row,
The fight was won but at what cost?
So many dead, so many lost,
But somehow beauty still prevails,
Here on Flanders fields.

Joseph Dunworth (10)

My Life As A Window

Myself cursed with immobility, wedged to these inescapable walls of injustice. How cruel may the heavens above be to cage me like this? How naive may the foreseers be to curse me upon this. I have no eyes to cry, but I still watch. I have no mouth to scream, but I still understand. I have no nose to sniffle, but I can sense the sorrow seeping out of the building, the screams and shouts of past memories. But then a thought came to me like a fly that can't see me: what was I made for? An impossible shiver came through my very being.

Never has there been a crueller time than now, the past of the future never to be spoken of. I see evil itself, I hear screams of pain and for mercy, I sense that I have witnessed something unjust, but I can no longer feel anything, my time has come. As time goes on, no one will remember me, no one will cry, no one will care; this is my life as a window.

Lucas Watkins (11)

Is It Meant To Be?

I don't wanna say goodbye, 'cause this one means forever
Dun, dun, dun, dun, dun, dun, dun, dun, dun
I don't wanna die all alone I just want you in my zone
100 miles away from home.
You are the one for me
Oh, oh, ooh, oh, oh, oh
Could it be maybe
Maybe it's not meant to be
You know I know, you know I know
Calling you on my phone
Oh, oh, ooh, oh, oh, oh
Never thought of this ending
Oh, oh, ooh, oh, oh, oh
Could it be maybe
Maybe
If you gave me a chance to breathe
Who knows the mysteries
And how we breathe
Could it be you and me
Who knows?
Are you the one for me?

You know I know
You know I know
You know I know
Oh, oh, ooh, oh, oh, oh
Just a confused girl with lots of history
You know I know, I know
Hey, hey, hey
Do you believe in me...

Liyan Omer (9)

Robbie The Robot

Walking up to an abandoned house,
Reggie sneaks in as quiet as a mouse.
He knows exactly what he saw,
And it was right behind this door.
It was fast, strong and had laser eyes,
But not very good at being in disguise.
The door opens with a loud creak,
Reggie turns his head to have a peek.
There he is shiny and white,
With his eyes beaming bright.
Was it real or was it not?
It really was a robot.
The two became very best friends,
Hoping their friendship never ends.
They'd go on adventures and teleport,
And even play all kinds of sport.
"Can you stay on Earth forever?"
The robot replied, "I'll leave you never."
Reggie was happy, jumping with joy,
It was like he had his own real-life toy.

"Robot, do you have a name?"
The robot put his head down in shame.
"Don't be sad, you're with me,
I will call you Robbie."

Reggie Stephens (8)

Possibilities

Perfect - it doesn't need to be, what matters is what we see
Opportunities await, just make sure you're not too late
Self-confidence is what we're looking for, knowing yourself even more
Satisfy your heart - do what it wants, act smart.
Ideally, make sure it's the right choice - you have a voice, make some noise.
Boundaries, no such thing, take the lead and be your king.
Innovation is a priority; sometimes you must make use of curiosity.
Leveraging is key, go ahead and set your thoughts free
Imagination is crucial, let it go wild and feel special
Try your best, pass the test and feel better than the rest
Inspiration is major, be an engager, then a creator
Exploring also won't bore you, more than half think it's true
So, what did you decide on - the easy and one-way path or the smarter and harder path?

Aishah Mohiuddin (11)

Sunshine Forever

Every summer I feel so excited because I go to Italy. My dad's hometown is Pescina. It is a small town up in the mountains, like a little ant on an anthill. On our journey to Pescina, I see layers of mountains as high as clouds. The clouds seem to be multiple witch hats that cover their heads.

The best time is when I meet my grandparents. I don't see them often, but having grandparents is special because I create unique memories with them. I feel over the moon, like scoring a bicycle kick at the final.

In Pescina, it is very busy. Our lives run as fast as Usain Bolt on the track because we want to enjoy every moment.

I am lucky that I have best friends in Pescina and in Manchester.

When it is time to go home, I feel sad and my heart breaks into pieces... but then I think that we will come back next year and so I start smiling again!

Leonardo Parisse (8)

The Dragon Beneath The Books

Beneath the shelves, beyond the dust,
Where no one looks and cobwebs rust,
A dragon sleeps with pages curled,
The quiet keeper of the world.

She feeds on tales that time forgot,
Half-finished dreams, a scribbled plot,
The final line that none knew,
The bedtime book you once outgrew.

She does not hoard the golden kind,
She keeps the stories left behind.
The ones that cracked or flew too wide,
Or slipped away before they died.

She warms them with her embered breath
And reads the lines I once left,
When the silence starts to creep,
She stirs and dreams begin to leap,

So if you lose a tale one day,
Just leave it where the stories stay,
Beneath the shelves, beyond the box,
For down below with silent grace,
The dragon keeps a timeless pace.

Aleena Hasan (10)

This Is My Season

This is my season,
This time it's spring,
Pink, yellow, green and blue all around you,
Daisies blooming everywhere for me and you to pick and share,
The rain is falling, let's run,
This is so much fun.

This is my season,
This time it's summer,
Ice cream in the sun, yum in my tum!
Quick, let's jump in the pool because it's time to get cool,
Butterflies and bees on the flowers, spending time outside for hours.

This is my season,
This time it's autumn,
Colourful leaves are falling down, grass all around,
Muddy puddles on windy walks,
Lots of hugs and happy talks.

This is my season,
This time it's winter,
Frosty snowflakes floating down,
Santa is coming, joy all around,
All these seasons, all done, we had lots of fun.

Pippa Young (8)

The Naughty Koala

I was in my room playing until I heard a sound.
It came from a box and *boom,* it came to the ground.
There was a rustle and a bustle and there was a click.
The box opened and a cute koala jumped out of it.
The koala was destroying the place.
"He's destroying my curtains, he's destroying my toys and he destroyed my Lego boy."
My mum came in my room with a shocked face.
She shouted, "Who did this?" And I gave her a mysterious face.
She brought me a broom
And said, "Clean your room."
I started to clean until I heard a bash,
"Oh no," I shouted, "my vase." *Crash!*
"Koala, don't be so mean."
The koala listened and decided to clean.
The koala finally listened
And now I could sleep while the moon glistened.

Victoria Wencel (10)

My Little Dog Spark

I have a little dog and his name is Spark.
For such a small dog, he has the loudest bark.
He loves to go on sunny walks,
With his wagging tail and bouncy paws.

He sniffs every blade of grass
With his tiny button nose.
Then he goes home for a long doze.

When he wakes up, he does a ginormous yawn,
Before nudging me to say, "Come on!"

Later on, in the afternoon,
His dinner is served in his favourite bowl.
He licks it clean until he can see his face -
All cute and cuddly, ready for a race.
He does zoomies until he starts to pant,
Then cocks his leg up a plant!

My little dog Spark goes off to bed,
Curls up in a ball and cuddles Mr Ted.
Then he lets out a little bark to say,
"What a good day I have had today."

Cerys Jones (8)

Autumn Delights

As swirling, colourful leaves descend like a feather from the high-top trees,
Squirrels scurry and gather nuts, as robins tweet merrily,
Further down, hedgehogs bury deep under the ground as hibernation will soon begin.
As we rake the crisp leaves that are bright orange, dull red and gold that look bold.
You can hear the whistling wind blow through your hair and feel the cool breeze softly passing by.
Acorns, rough pinecones and smooth conkers fall nearby the busy market that sells spices.
Around the season, we harvest giant pumpkins, crunchy carrots, juicy apples and tasty plums.
Toffee apple is a good treat that is sweet.
As dawn turns to dusk, you can smell wood smoke nearby the crackling fire.
As the season comes to an end, we get cosy and snug in our blankets by our warm, toasty fireplace.

Meera Sivarajah (8)

Melodies

Music is my thing.
I like it,
I play the violin!
If I... tumble, trip or my instrument slips,
No matter what happens, I'll never lose it!
Music is my thing.
I like it,
I play the piano!
I'll play, play, play, play, play all day;
Press with my fingers and shout hooray!
Music is my thing.
I like it,
I play the flute!
I'll whistle, not whimper right into the chute,
For I love my instrument, my dear little flute!
Music can lift our spirits high, high, high.
It's lovely and melodic, pretty as the sky.
It might even feel as though you could fly!
So go hear some music, whether it's pop or rock.
Sing and dance to it and hop to the top!
Music is our thing,
We like it, and together we sing!

Isabel Orozco Matabuena (9) & Satya Misztal (9)

Yeah, Summer Is Here!

Summer is here with full gear.
Scent of pleasing lavender and BBQ in the air.

The temperature is soaring
But the owls are snoring.

It's nice and bright
Great weather to fly your kite.

Everyone is splashing in the pool
To make their bodies cool.

People are hitting the gym
To get absolutely slim.

Magnificent time to have a BBQ
Without fussing in the queue.

Epic moment for some freezing pint of ice cream
Topped with chocolate chips and caramel cream.

On the golden sandy beach,
Relax and have some peach.

A long summer day with plenty of hours to play.
I wish they would always stay.

Time to sleep, let's turn on the fan.
Gear up in pyjamas and ride on the dreamy van.

Omar Faisal (10)

The Dark Side Of London

London, London, a city of crime...
London, London, no extra time...
If they have a knife...
They will take your life...
They will murder your wife...
The government... What will they do?
Nothing is true,
Who will they sue?
No one will care,
Until he's there,
Right in front of their own witnessing eyes,
You will hear cries until somebody dies,
It's a really high chance,
The experience,
You can cry, you can try, you can die,
The sympathy is gone by tea,
Your dead body is all they see,
They will say sorry. What will we do?
There are many cases just like you...

London... a lost cause,
London... no laws,
London... full of crime,
London... they will end your time...
They will lend you to your end.

Abdulrahman Shah (11)

The Taiga

Magical, beautiful, glimmering,
Blankets of snow shimmering,
The most stunning biome,
Where wonderful animals freely roam.

Majestic, captivating lakes,
Consuming, blizzarding snowflakes,
Towering evergreen trees,
Swaying in the glacial breeze.

Home to the peacefully hibernating bear,
Few animals withstand the harsh, icy air,
Reindeer fleeing in fear,
Deforestation is near.

Humans are the world's biggest threat,
This place is one we can't forget,
With soil erosion, forest fires and mining,
Animals are left crying and dying.

Let's stop fossil fuel extraction,
It is essential we take action,
In order for this world to survive,
We must let the Taiga thrive.

Mati Allen (12)

The Sand Queen

She lurks between the shadows,
Casting many spells.
She catches my eye within the forest,
Jamming my humble dwell.
My solemn days, not so bright,
Gives me a gigantic fright.
The memories of myself
Never used me as much as when she broke inside my shell.
Why, oh why did she have to be so eerie?
Maybe if I ran away, she wouldn't catch me so speedily.
I run and run, and still no sight.
I wipe the sweat off my forehead,
Wishing for a serene night.
The queen, dressed in fancy attire
And a golden sparkly crown.
I saw her kind of staring at me,
As she held her silver gown.
She looked at me as if she was trying to tell me,
Run away.
But I looked at her as
If she was trying to lead me astray.

Minha Rehman (10)

Play, Play, Play

Play, play, play,
Axolotls sing and swim their song all day.

Pearls, pearls, wonderful pearls,
In their shells they twirl and swirl.

Shells communicate, shells sing.
Their delightful voice sounds like a dream
And when they communicate
It is nice to hear their melody once or twice.

The kelp waves through the sand
And the waves wave like a hand.

Camouflaged axolotls swim safe and sound
Away from the predators that are around.

Axolotls play, play, play,
They play until the day has shone.

Yawn, yawn, yawn,
Time for bed as another day will come.

The waves wave through this land
As they dream in the sleepy sand.

Night, night little ones.

Lotte Slijboom (8)

Threads Of Friendship

In the quiet of life's ebb and flow,
A beacon shines, a steady glow.
Through tempest winds and skies turned grey.
Friendship dawns, a bright array.
A hand extended, firm and true,
A laugh that breaks the clouds in two.
Its roots run deep, its branches wide,
A shelter found where hearts confide.
Time may weather and seasons change,
Yet the bond remains, unchanged.
Through whispered secrets, joys and tears,
A tapestry woven through the years.
Not bound by blood, but by the soul,
Each thread stitched makes us whole.
A gift, unpriced, yet rich indeed,
A friend fulfils life's quiet need.
So, cherish well this golden thread,
Its warmth, its light, till journey's end.
For in its embrace, we find our part,
A friend, a mirror to the heart.

Lucy Gipters (9)

My Adventures!

I came across a haunted house,
That I stumbled on my way.
I opened the door to a large grey mouse,
In fright, I ran away.
The next day, I went to the woods,
To find some buried treasure.
I found it under a bundle of hoods,
The stash was not to my pleasure.
One week later, I went to sea,
To find a sunken ship.
Then I found a little dolphin with a face full of glee.
It swam to a very big dip.
One month later, I went into a cave,
To battle with a dragon.
I was in armour and was very brave,
Just to face an empty wagon.
One year later, I went to a castle,
That was on a steep hill.
Then, I felt something that gave me a chill,
So I went to the top without any hassle.
Just as I stopped to admire the scene,
I felt like I was a queen!

Esha Raheel (11)

Love Dogs Today Forever

L ove for life,
O live for a name,
V oting for a dog,
E very little bit of rain.

D ogs and people make good friends with Asha,
Penny and Emily.
O lives are not tasty for dogs mostly,
G eography for dogs, maybe no,
S cience, too much exploding.

T o make and bake,
O lives to cook.
D ads make jokes,
A uthors make books,
Y apping is yapping.

F loors are clean,
O lives are cooked,
R oofs are clean,
E very little bit,
V ery warm or cold, you're the best dog in the world,
E njoyment for the
R elationship with dogs.

Sarah Smart (9)

Halloween

Halloween is creepy,
Dangerously freaky,
Trick or treat,
Stealing sweets
Clueless about danger and zombies galore,
This night is completely free of sunny verdure,
For down here monsters lurk,
Through the dark night, witches skulk.
The skeletons wide-awake, avoiding their graves,
With them around no one will ever be brave,
Ghosts dormant and moaning and wishing for life,
They get it once a year on Halloween night
You seek a miracle,
Only finding me to be lyrical,
You need an escape,
From this treacherous gothic place,
But, alas, there is none,
Time cannot be undone,
We are condemned to a dark and horrific night,
Once a year, we suffer this plight,

Halloween is creepy,
Dangerously freaky,
Trick or treat,
Stealing sweets.

Suhana Rajan (12)

A Cave

I am the ghostly silence,
Haunting all who enter,
I'm nothing but death and violence,
The all-mighty dementor.

I am as dark as an eye sealed shut,
Echoes like a basketball bouncing off the wall,
The whimper of forgotten souls fills your head,
The never-ending fear turns your run to a crawl.

I am like the mouth of a sleeping giant, waiting to snore,
The air as still as the most terrible secrets,
Possessing ghosts make you tumble to the floor,
The shrill cry of hidden spirits.

I am as cold as a freezer of long-buried icicles,
My water as rough and ancient as dragon skin,
Within my walls lie extinct life-cycles,
None will return who wander in.

Milo Cronshaw (10)

The Little Robot

Hi my name is Robo,
I like to play with magic,
I don't want to mess anything up,
Or it would be rather tragic.

My favourite colour is purple,
It's strange for a robot I know,
But I don't care what anyone thinks,
So up and away I go.

I'm up in the clouds now,
It's really calm up here,
Now let's play with magic,
And make purple particles appear.

Oh no, my magic's all gone wrong,
The clouds have all turned purple,
Now the whole world will turn that colour,
And I'm in a lot of trouble.

I don't know what to do,
Maybe add that and this,
The purple is now all gone,
Into the great abyss.

Seren Parkinson (9)

The Tulips

Based on 'The Daffodils' by William Wordsworth

I wandered lonely as a cloud
That drifts high over hills and mountains
But then I saw a bright crowd,
A host of golden tulips
Beside the sparkling lake beneath the willow trees,
Gently fluttering and dancing in the breeze.

Continous as stars that shine
And twinkle on the Milky Way,
They stretched along the lake's shore in a never-ending line
Standing tall on their green stems
With one glance, I saw thousands of them
Feeling their heads in a cheerful dance.

Their heads glowing lightly like the sun
Petals slightly closed but open
I sat on the grass
Watching the starry night
The waves wiggled gently
As I admired the beautiful view.

Sophie Warzala (10)

The Most Adorable Animal In The World

The most adorable animal in the world,
Is not a lamb with its fleece all curled,
Or a rabbit always jumping,
With its feet constantly thumping.
It's not a fish drinking, drinking,
Nor a frog always thinking,
Guinea pigs pooping pebbles,
Lions are constant rebels.
An axolotl may play dead,
A dog would rest its sleepy head,
Cat? No, but you're close,
With water it needs a small dose.
A kitten, yes! It's super soft,
Keeping all your hopes aloft,
Very cuddly and cute,
Catching birds that hoot, hoot.

It's cute, it's true,
A silky feel for you,
With its slinky tail curled,
It's the most adorable animal in the world.

Ophelia Shaw (10)

A Day At The Park

Start our day in the park today,
Meet our friends and laugh and play.
To the playground, we make our way,
Start the fun with one big sway.
On the swing we float and fly,
Feet reach up to touch the sky.
It might be fun to slide today,
So to the slide we run, hooray!
The monkey bars call our name,
Each swing is a part of our game.
Imagination starts to roar.
We race, we chase, we jump, we spin,
Letting all the laughter in.
The sun shines bright, the sky is blue.
The day is made for me and you.
As moon is showing and sunlightened,
We wave goodbye to all our friends,
The park's fun will come another day,
But how great was this day's play?

Emma Waseem (10)

My Dragon And Me

My dragon likes to scorch the emerald grass with flames
I tell them not to burn my toes

My dragon likes to loop-the-loop high up in the sky
I tell them not to drop me

My dragon likes to crunch peppercorns
I tell them not to sneeze on me

My dragon likes to boast that they are the strongest
I tell them not to show off, or the other dragons will challenge them

My dragon likes to steal shiny treasure
I tell them not to, or the police will come

My dragon likes to chew my shoes
I tell them not to make big holes, or I won't be able to go to school

My dragon likes to fly off
I tell them not to leave me
I love them so much.

Alex Jennings-Moore (9)

Nutella Goodness

Oh, beautiful Nutella, I love you so,
You're my favourite breakfast spread,
I go from tired to a wide-awake glow
When I spread you thickly on my bread!

My friends and family like peanut butter
But they haven't got a clue,
You make my heart race and flutter,
But peanut spread tastes like salty glue.

On a cool cucumber, I love you most,
The combination sends me to the moon,
My friends just think that's weird and gross,
But that brown and green, it makes me swoon.

Your silk and gloss are a lake of joy, a treasure, pure gold, my hazel jewel,
You light me up, I am a rocket flying to the stars and you are my comfort fuel.

Emily Boo Henry-Hogg (9)

Wonderverse

In the ocean deep down,
Whales jump out with a big splash onto belly,
They protect their little ones teaching pride and joy,
They splish and plop down, down and down.

In the ocean deep down,
Seahorses drift around,
Having fun in the most charming way,
They stay at the bottom while the men carry babies.

In the ocean deep down,
Jellyfish wiggle and swirl,
Among the colourful coral and swaying seaweed,
They float with a gentle glide,
A lovely sight in the ocean's light.

In the ocean deep down,
Sharks swim around with their fins poking out,
They rule the sea both day and night,
They hunt for their prey fiercely.

Emily Martin (8)

Every Single Day

I stare out my window every single day,
Imagining lands really far away.
Lands with big horses,
Jumping some really terrifying courses.
Lands with really huge shops,
And most sell the best lollipops.

I stare at my toys every single day,
And imagine lands that are brilliant to play.
Lands about a girl at school,
Who is pretty cool.
Lands with unicorns,
That love, love, love prawns.

I stare at my bookshelf every single day,
Imagining what land to read today.
Lands about knights,
Who fly kites.
Lands about dogs,
Who have friends that are frogs.

But every single day,
I give my mum a hug, like today.

Annie Conlon (9)

Exploring The Universe

I want to be an explorer!
That's all I want to do,
I want to be an explorer,
One day my dream will come true.

I want to travel the ocean
And swim with the waves,
I want to see some sharks,
So I'll go through some underwater caves.

I want to explore the jungle
And spot a lake,
That glimmers in the sun,
But I'll have to be aware of the poisonous snake!

I want to travel to space
And see all the stars,
I'll make a wish,
I'll make it on Mars.

I want to go to the desert
And put my bare feet on the sand,
I want to visit every desert
And visit every land.

Aadhya Shah (8)

A Day In May

Winds are windy and clouds are cloudy
Skies are blue and cows go moo
Deep down where the clouds are grey
Came an old chap, who was coming to stay

Far away where rain meets pain
It was an old hut with fruits as its main
And hey, the chap was coming to stay

In a lair, short and cute
A man was coming their way
The day was grey and the sky made way
For a hot air balloon with a chap who was coming to stay
Said, "Make way, make way"
For this man was like no other
He was thin as a pancake
His eyes were like the beads in your necklace
He was coming to stay
What would you do if you came in May?

Hayyan Badoordeen (10)

Turtle The Tortoise

I want a turtle pet
But a tortoise is all I get.
It turns out tortoises are really funny
And he is sweet as honey.

Mischievous and amusing,
This tortoise is very confusing.
Sometimes he bumps into glass windows
And opens cupboards with his nose - oh no!

He seems to be always smiling
Even when he is sliding on the tiling.
He's clumsy, he's sleepy and also sneaky,
Turns my homework to pieces - how cheeky!

When he goes up the stairs
He pulls his legs in pairs.
And then backwards he folds
And the feet in the air he holds.

I want a turtle pet
But a tortoise is all I get.

Afonso Casanova (9)

Poem

The eldest was born,
She grew up as fast as dawn,
Then another baby came as cute as his name,
He was Kai Kai and he was the second born,
Evaan came next,
He was the best to make you laugh,
The fourth was Naomi, born with eyes like the sky,
Was a gift from God sent down from high.

They all like to celebrate their funny side,
In public or inside,
No matter what they ever do,
They're happy because they've got them too.

After all,
Across the land,
Across the sea,
Together their hearts will always be.

Forever together and never apart,
This love they share conquers four hearts.

Hana Virdee (10)

Read With Nature

R ead and wander through the wood
E xplore each leaf like Red Riding Hood
A perfect sunny day where flowers grow
D rift through pages, soft and slow.

W atch the seasons turn and spin
I magine a world of fiction both out and in
T rees stand tall with whispered lore
H ear the wind through nature's door.

N estled in peace the ink hums
A ir like breath through ancient drums
T urn each page like petals bloom
U nder branches, stories loom
R oots of thought and bark of rhyme
E lectronically hooked, keep reading through time.

Safiya Ali (10)

Spring Wakes The Earth

Spring wakes the earth
No footsteps tread where moss has grown,
Yet life returns, unsummoned sown.
A shiver thawing ground,
And roots begin their soft rebound.

Bud by bud, the branches rise,
Sketching green against wide skies.
Rain taps gently, leaf to stone,
Each drop a voice the woods have known.

In quiet marsh, the frogs begin,
Their echoes round the reed skin,
Cloud drifts slow with silver threads,
Above the hills where colour spreads.

No names are carved on breeze or bark,
No witness signs the meadow's spark,
Yet still comes, without decree,
This blooming hush of mystery.

Sara Foughali (10)

Wartime

Darkness, that is all I could see. As I hit random buttons, I could hear booming outside. *Boom! Bang! Crash!*
I could hear the screams of men being shot to the ground, suffering a painful and slow death.
I could hear trees falling down, making massive holes in the ground.
I could hear soldiers from both sides battling to their deaths, like it was the last thing they would ever do.
There was one soldier I could hear; he sounded like he was right next to me, begging me for help. And there I was, in my sanctuary of safety. My tank. Helpless. Weak. A wave of guilt washed over me. But what was I to do? Other than hear them all suffer and cry out for me in pain.

Shayna Pancholi (11)

The Dull Island

There's an island far away,
Where the sun forgets to play.
No waves to crash, no birds that sing,
Just silence, and the cold winds bring.

The trees are bare, the sky is grey,
The air feels heavy night and day.
The ground is dry, no flowers bloom,
Just endless fog – no light, no room.

No friendly sound, no fun, no cheer,
Just lonely whispers in the air.
I sit and stare, but there's no spark,
The island's dull, lost in the dark.

I dream of colours bright and bold,
Of places warm, not wet and cold.
But here I wait with nothing new,
A dull island with skies so blue.

Noah Dawood

Inside The Mind Of An Illustrator

Inside the mind of an illustrator,
It is magical and amazing,
There are mountains as tall as skyscrapers
And rivers that stretch further than your dreams.
Dragons that roam the skies,
Clouds that you can fly on,
For inside the mind of an illustrator,
It's creative and wondrous, fantastic and beautiful,
Inventive and artistic,
Because inside the mind of an illustrator,
It has to be full of amazing ideas,
But, inside the mind of an illustrator,
It can be dangerous, petrifying and deadly,
So be careful when you look,
Even peek inside,
For inside the mind of an illustrator,
Anything could happen.

Esme Farnden (10)

The End

M inecraft mobs are dreadful and petrifying
I n the End, you face a fierce dragon with purple eyes
N ever give up while dodging its poisonous purple fireballs
E nder pearls can be crafted into eyes of Ender, which lead to the End
C rafting tools can lead you to the pitch-black Nether, where danger lies around every corner
R afting in the Overworld is complicated, but boating is simple
A pples aren't very filling and they're tough to find
F inding cobblestone is easy - just dig and mine the stone you uncover
T urn on Peaceful Mode and play free from the mobs and their terror!

Oliver Gladwin (8)

My Sister

My sister is my partner in every single way,
She's a star in my life,
Come what may,
Her laughter is a melody that is beautiful and clear,
Her presence is what makes the world feel near.
Through thick and thin,
She's by my side,
She's a constant support,
My endless pride.
Our love is too strong,
For anybody to refuse,
She is the lighter
And I am the fuse.
If you weren't there, in this world,
I don't know what I'd do.
I'll be lost in an empty place
Stuck, without you.
Her spirit is fierce, but tender and kind
I love her a lot, she's a treasure I find!

Mukta Kulkarni (10)

Mournful Morning

Waking up is always annoying,
Yet another mournful morning.

The clouds are so dim,
The sun has gone in.
Children are sleeping,
Babies are weeping.

Yet another mournful morning.

Dogs are howling,
Cats are growling.
The wind starts blowing,
Dawn begins showing.

Yet another mournful morning.

Rats are sneaking,
Children start peeking.
Leaves start falling,
Morning's calling.

Yet another mournful morning.

Doves are cooing,
Coffee's brewing.
Dishwashers shaking,
Beds need making.

Yet another mournful morning!

Avie Combes (9)

My Bike

I like to ride my bike
I ride up and down the road.
The wind rushing past
Although my wheel is slightly bowed!

I like to ride my bike
And ride it up the ramps.
My mum thinks it's so scary
It makes her start to dance!

I like to ride my bike
I ride it to the shop.
A newspaper for Mr Edwards
And for me, a bottle of pop!

I like to ride my bike
I ride it to the park.
I ride it over the mole hills
Must get back before it's dark!

I like to ride my bike
I ride it with my friends.
I'm glad I have a big brother
Who fixes it when it needs amends!

Solomon Salisbury (9)

Baby, Can You Clap?

Inspired by 'Gran Can You Rap?' by Jack Ousby

My baby was in her cot she was taking a nap
When I poked her to see if she could clap
Baby can you clap, clap, clap, clap, can you?
She smiled at me with her big, brilliant, brown eyes and said to me,
"Bro! I'm the best clapping baby this world's ever seen
I'm a boo boo, ba ba, goo goo, ga ga clapping queen."

She clapped down the stairs with a yee hee
Into the garden tippity tap towards the tree
She clapped past me and my little sister
And clapped past our pet hamster Glister
She clapped up the hill
What a thrill
I'm a clip clap, pit pat, rip rap
Clapping crazy baby.

Abdullah Haqani (8)

The Unicorn That Saves The Day

Darkness fell, the woods so cold,
A scary story to be told.
But then a light, a horn so bright,
A unicorn, pure and white!

The shadows hissed, they could not stay,
The unicorn bravely chased them away.
Its magical horn, a shining spear,
Brought back the sunshine, banished fear.

The animals cheered, the day was new,
Thanks to the magic, strong and true,
Of the unicorn brave and bold,
Whose shining story will be told.

The flowers woke, the birds took flight,
The woods were happy, filled with light.
Of the unicorn's gentle grace,
As light returned to that dark place.

Sanithree Nuweena Herath Mudiyanselage (10)

When I Grow Up

When I grow up, I want to be happy like a winner, like a baby being sung a lullaby, like a child with ice cream, positive, joyful with glee.

When I grow up, I want to be as powerful as an actor, like a president making laws, rising high and strong.

When I grow up, I want to be talented like an Oscar winner getting trophies and awards, an Olympic medal winner getting handed the gold medal, an award winner special and creative.

When I grow up, I want to be successful like a millionaire, like a fashion designer, loved, popular and famous.

When I grow up, I will be happy, powerful, talented. I will be me.

Alanna Griffiths (10)

Me And My Unicorn

I once met a unicorn,
One beyond compare.
One with a golden horn,
A mane like Rapunzel's hair.

I was sitting in the forest.
She came up to me and neighed.
I may not be a folklorist,
But she wasn't afraid.

She was all alone.
Nobody to love.
She had been unknown.
She was a mourning dove.

I loved her with all my heart.
She was my best friend.
But then we had to part.
But this wasn't the end.

My unicorn and I
Will see each other again,
Even if I'm in the blissful sky.
I'll always know her by her mane.

Indigo Adkins (10)

Friendship

F riends make everyone happy
R eally warm inside is what my friends make me feel
I n arguments, friendship breaks, but they can come together again
E veryone could have an argument whether friends or not
N ever lie to a friend; they are only there to help
D on't just watch your friends being bullied, tell someone trusted
S ometimes friends seem closer and sometimes they seem further away
H appiness will always lead the way to friends
I n friendship, it makes you feel safe
P laying with friends will always make you smile.

Oralia Barton (9)

State Of Our Sea

We need to see the state of our sea -
The sea that once shimmered, bright and free,
The sea that used to look back at me.

But now, its beauty fades away,
Its brilliance dulls, its waves betray -
It no longer looks back at me.

I ask you now,
Will the next generation scream aloud?

Will you sit in your rocking chair,
As a child asks, unaware,
"What's that thing? Didn't it used to be blue?"

Will you let history recall our fate -
A generation meek, weak and late?

No.

It starts today.
Stand up, take this vow -
Come and see the state of our sea.

Ayesha Khan (12)

The Birds At The Park

Have you ever seen a bird at a park,
Swooping and soaring into the dark?
Flapping its wings, gliding so high,
Disappearing into the night sky,
Flying by the light of the moon.
I wonder if he'll come back soon?
Or is he hunting for his food?
"What will I do without you?" he said.

His beak as pointy as a hook,
Squawking with the food he took.
See him shimmering, see him cruising,
As far as he could.
Looping, somersaulting, flying to his nest.
He really is trying his best.
Hungry chicks squeaking and squawking
Throughout the night.

Isabelle Rose Davis (7)

Growing A Garden

I was strolling through the park,
When I suddenly fell through the path,
Into a place I still recall vividly.
Multiple patches of earth;
Some of which had exotic plants:
Bananas, beanstalks,
Mangoes and coconuts,
There was flora flourishing everywhere!
Then someone came up to me and said,
"Go buy some carrot seeds from the seed dealer,
And plant them to start your garden."

Soon enough, I had my exquisite fruits:
Pea pods, peppers,
Watermelons and pumpkins.
But as suddenly as I had fallen here,
I fell again,
And woke up.

Talha Myth (11)

Beyond The Horizon

Beyond the horizon,
Where dolphins glide,
Their movements swift and slow.
Where mermaids flick their shimmering tails,
Showing off all of their skills.
Where turtles flap their wrinkled flippers,
Blinking their wise old eyes.
Where jellyfish bob and wriggle,
Their fluorescent tentacles powering them along.

To golden sands full of treasure galore
And cities made of silver.
To countrysides full of emerald shrubs
And deserts lit by a burning sun.

Beyond the horizon.
Where magic becomes a reality
And dreams more than a fantasy.

Millie Beasley (10)

An Empty Void

S olar system surrounds us planets covering us in a warm blanket, our leader is a fireball that is scorching
P lanets are our home, we are never leaving, we care for our cow patch planet very much, it's home
A stronauts sent from home quite far away, we all salute them bravely, all we see is the smoky essence, goodbye.
C onstellations: myth or not? Creatures in the sky: reality or lies? Who really knows until you see it lie finally.
E arth, where crystal-clear, majestic water runs our place only, creatures dance and prance, a great pull brings us together.

Georgia Lane (10)

Riddle Me This

I have a bill but I am not a duck,
I have a flat tail but I am not a beaver,
I am venomous if I'm a male but not a snake,
I lay eggs if I'm female but I am not a bird,
I have waterproof fur but I am not a polar bear,
I have webbed limbs but I am not a puffin,
I have an unusual appearance but I am not a glass frog,
I don't have a stomach but I am not a ghost flower,
I have no teeth but I'm still not an anteater,
My animal's newborn is a puggle but I'm not an echidna.
Can you guess what I am?

Answer: I am a platypus.

Abdul Hannan (11)

Dinosaur

D eep green, scaly skin, like the bright summer leaves
of a palm tree.
I mmensely scary roar that will set it free.
N obody could beat the monstrous giants out of fear.
O ver the mountains, is where they live and they feed
on those that are near.
S piky, tall, short and long, they come in all different
forms.
A ngry creatures, known as terrible lizards, can also
fly within their norms.
U sed to rule the mighty world with their sharp fangs.
R ebellious friends, once the inhabitants met an
asteroid and went out with a bang!

Mohammed Ihaan (8)

Point Of View

It comes to all who have been born:
A perspective or a point of view.
From family, friends and much, much more,
A perspective or a point of view.

It changes by age all the time.
Like a house for instance,
With many windows to explore,
And as you gain in age, you'll discover many more
Points of view.

Experiences matter lots as well,
What you've done, how you excel.
It's all part of a perspective,
Or a point of view.

Perspective matters,
For all we think, say and do,
That's my point of view.

Isaac Smith (10)

The Natural World

Trees
Luscious leaves swaying,
Joyful children climbing,
Delicate branches waving,
Forever life giving.

Flowers
Iridescent rainbow,
Precious roses grow,
Glorious golds glow,
Forever life giving.

The Sea
Like a ferocious dragon the waves crash,
With a mighty roar, a sensational splash,
The turquoise waters smash,
Forever life giving.

Rivers
Majestic and moody, meandering
Like a diamond glistening...
With dozy ducks waddling,
Forever life giving.

Rosanna Wallace (9)

World Of Wonder

Look out and see the journey ahead
A world full of many mysteries to be made
You'll know when you've made a true discovery
And you'll want to share it with everyone too
So just open the door
Let the journey begin
And the curiosity fills within

For people who hold a sense of adventure
Come join us on our grand expedition
Bring family and friends
So that they can also encounter the many wonders
The adventure is waiting to be explored
Fun hiding in every clue
Why not be the ones to conquer this endless
adventure?

Inaaya Kashif (10)

The Bird Of Light

High in the sky, so beautiful and bright,
Swooping up and down both day and night.
Looking left and right with his striking eyes,
An eagle is about the same size.

His feathers so vibrant gold,
This fiery bird will never be cold.
The golden halo around his head,
This mythical creature can never be dead.

With his handsome feathered crest,
This bird is reborn out of his fiery nest.
From the ashes of the fire,
He then soars even higher.

This immortal phoenix bird,
Flies so fast he's all blurred.
This phoenix symbolises hope,
No matter what, it can cope.

Alice Birkinshaw (9)

Pollution

These animals are suffering on our Earth
These are what we see in life
From the depths of the earth to the end of life

We stand here letting animals suffer before our eyes
The oil in the water is poisoning our sea creatures

From life to death,
This is what we are currently seeing

This oil is causing penguins to be left to drown

"Treat animals as they would treat you"

Also, they would be losing heat,
Which means they would lose waterproofing
Which also lets them die in the depths of the sea.

Barakel Lartey (12)

Wonder

I wonder if the stars shine yellow.
I wonder if I can play the cello.
Sometimes I wonder if I could sing,
Or if I'll ever be king.
Myself may wonder if aliens are real,
Could the moon be something you steal?
Is it okay to be afraid of the dark,
Or take a gigantic stroll in the park?
If adults can turn little again,
And kids could turn magically into a pen.
If everyone in the world wore glasses.
Can people take millions of dashes?
People's eyesight turned into green.
I finally wonder if there's a time machine.

Cynara Benjamin (10)

The Highland Phantom

The glassy, sleek crescent moon bathed the mountain range in a pearlescent cloak.
The cluster of alps, hidden by scree, were gorged by a cobalt rapid, with an estuary at the northernmost point of the range.
Gale weathered the alpine meadow, yet the mountains loomed, forbiddingly over the gust.
Upon the craggy ledges, tulips, snowdrops, roses all grew tall and prosperous.
The roots of the mountains grew slowly deeper with every hour that passed.
Crevices wounded the towering pinnacle, which was veiled by clouds blown down to Earth by celestials.

Ben Payne (10)

The Wonders Of Nature

The leaves wave goodbye on the trees,
The soft wind blows them away.
Where will they wander to?
"Goodbye to the leaves," I say.

Daisies blow in the air,
The sunflowers do the same.
It's like they love to dance,
That must be what's brought their fame.

The trees wiggle their arms,
As if to say hello.
A man walks past,
They must be talking to the fellow.

The nature is so soothing,
Calm and amazing.
What is nature?
Well, it's not a thing, it's amazing.

Sophia Henrietta Mallorie-Little (10)

Today

Today the sun is shining so bright and the lush,
green grass is waving side to side,
while the fresh, sweet wind is moving from one place to another.

Birds are chirping, singing their beautiful song.
Gorillas are smashing like King Kong.
Aliens are looking for their friend.
Mailmen are all ready to send.

My sister is typing and my mum is writing.
My sister is learning while Dad is messaging.
I am thinking while Mum is blinking.
I went to the post office
And then I noticed that the puppy in front of me was the softest.

Kaylen Pancholi (8)

Seasons

Winter
Winter is here,
It is the best season of the year,
It is time to clap and cheer,
Yay, winter is here.

Spring
Ding, dong, ding
It is finally spring,
The robins go away
And the swallows are here to stay.

Summer
It is finally summer,
The hottest season of the year,
Go down to the beach
And perhaps eat a peach.

Autumn
Autumn leaves falling everywhere,
I want to go outside, look and stare.

Sofia Lumley (8)

Swallow

I wheel through the misty morning air
Nobody notices, not that I care
The clouds above turn from white to grey
And I head straight into the fray.

A torrent of rain comes lashing down
For I had flown into the storm of dread renowned
Hour after hour I flew
And suddenly the sky turned blue.

But still on I went -
Time and energy I spent
I got tired and so did the sun
It climbed into cosy red covers like a little'un

And so it was time for bed
I landed in a hollow tree
And as for tomorrow -
Well, wait and see.

Henry Page (10)

Nature

A place where you can let your inner thoughts roam
Some may call it home
It is a place full of beauty
It is like being in a movie
Where everything seems too good to be true

Plants and vines growing everywhere
I could be anywhere
But I choose to be here
Every day, every year

Nature is everywhere
No matter if you're in a town
Or even a house
So turn your frown upside down
And open your eyes to the nature around you
Even if it is as small as a mouse.

Syeda Anisa Mumtaz Nakvi (11)

The Princess Was A Hero And Saved The Day

There once was a lovely princess
With a very long, frilly pink dress.
She was always charming,
Which is quite alarming,
She also likes to play a lot of chess.

There once was a wizard called Wally,
He was always very jolly.
He could cast a great spell,
Wally turned mean as well,
He had a large spider called Holly.

Wally set fire to a house,
He always wore a little blouse.
Princess saved the day
And started to slay away,
He was gone as quick as a mouse.

Lily McCormick (8)

Gondahoos

Everyone nowadays always takes the trees for granted,
But if you look closer, the trees are enchanted!
There on the bark, little people thrive,
Yes, I know, they are alive!
All the little men and women build houses every day,
Then all the little boys and girls say,
"Hooray, hoorah, another house added today,
Now that another house is built, we can stop and say...
let's play!"
And that's the story of the gondahoos.
But now this has to end, or else they'll see me toos!

Eliana Munday (9)

A Poem About Poetry

A single word upon the page,
A single performer on the stage,
A single idea in a brilliant mind,
Something beautiful you can find.

A poem is heard, a poem is seen,
A poem is blue, a poem is green,
A poem is here, a poem is there,
Shared by everyone, everywhere.

The flame that never dies,
The water that never dries,
The air that's never breathed,
The earth that grows the seeds.

It's everything we use,
It's everything we lose,
It's everything we see,
It's everything we breathe.

Jessica Luke (11)

The Witch's Daughter

Once upon a time, there was a witch called Criecre. There was also a teenage blonde boy called Arctus in a nearby village. He was like the village hero.
One day, he was out on a walk when he saw Chiloe, Criecre's daughter (he didn't know she was a witch) and said hi.
She said hi too and they walked together. They started to form a relationship. As they reached a fire, Criecre said, "I didn't want to have to do this." Then, she pushed Arctus in. Arctus vanished into the fire, never to be seen again.

Olivia Dodimead (10)

Scarlett Hero

My car is magical!
I am sure it can fly!
Like a superhero flying high in the sky.
I have named the car Scarlett Hero
Mummy asks if I have named it after Captain Scarlett
"No," I say.
Our Skoda is red, scarlet red!
It can save us all from the baddies in the world
Three cheers for Scarlett Hero!
Hip, hip hooray!
Hip, hip hooray!
Hip, hip hooray!
My car is wonderful
It takes me to places where rockets soar and volcanoes erupt!
Thank you, Scarlett Hero.

Rae Jackson (7)

The Mystery House

One day, two boys, Mark and Paul, were walking along a road. Suddenly, a house that said, "Come in," appeared in front of them! It was as if they were under a spell because they found themselves walking in the house! In the house, they found food and a postcard that said 'Eat well'.
After the long walk, they could almost eat anything. Paul touched the food and a witch appeared. They ran while the witch chased them. They called for help and a woodcutter came, hit her with an axe and she died!

Muhammad Rana (8)

My Animal Riddles

My animal has long hair
And big, cute eyes with a wiggly piglet nose.
Kids like to see it because it looks nice.
The colour is pink and yellow like a meadow.
What is it?

Answer: A pony.

Hop, hop, hop,
I am white and grey, soft and fluffy, cuddly and cute.
What am I?

Answer: A rabbit.

I walk on all fours,
I have a furry tail and sharp claws and whiskers.
What am I?

Answer: A kitten.

Hannah Daya

The Candy World

T ime is not real here,
H eather the elf is here!
E verything is made of candy and chocolate.

N ever go to the marshmallow wizard!
E very day you will meet someone new
W hen night comes the sugar fairies come out to play

W ater is made out of sweet chocolate,
O h the sweet smell in the air
R are things can be found around here
L etters are made out of paper wafers
D o have some candy!

Luca Devenney (8)

The Boy And Space

Once there was a little boy called Mark. He was seven and he lived on a canal boat and he was left alone as usual.
Mark found a shark in a swimming pool next to his park.
Luna, his sister, always went out to the nearby tuna shop owned by Moon-a.
Sunny, his younger brother, bought a bunny for free, so he didn't need money. Everyone said his tummy was so funny.
In space, Clair didn't like it because she lost all of her hair and didn't wear a pair of shoes and had nothing to share.

Milo Leal-Rice

Our Best Friends - Our Pets

Our little friends,
The ones to snug up to,
The lifesavers,
The best.

Our furry friends
The ones,
The ones who stick,
Who stick with you through the good and bad.

Our slimy friends,
The ones who just shed their skin,
The ones who Mum and Dad forgot to feed,
Forgot to feed while you were away.

So please can we,
Can we love them,
Even if they bark or bite?
Because let's face it, they are man's best friend.

Ethan Davis (12)

The Forest

The forest is awakening,
I smell some baking.
The trees are swishing,
The world is wishing.
The birds are singing,
the children are winning.
The leaves are crunching,
The boxers are punching.
The flowers are growing,
The gardeners mowing.
The hares are running,
The foxes are cunning.
The deer are eating,
The parents are meeting.
The sun goes down,
The king's getting crowned.
The forest is sleeping,
The bed is greeting.

Iris Stapleton Smith (8)

The Demanding Rhyme

Once upon a time,
There was a demanding rhyme
Saying, "Save the planet,"
Before it crumbles like pulverised granite,
Deforestation,
Is a very bad situation!
Littering the ground,
Soon, there will be no animals to be found!
Polluting the sea,
It'll be gone in a jiffy...
You think it doesn't affect our health,
Soon, there will be no air to breathe!
I recommend listening to this demanding rhyme,
Before we run out of time.

Rayyan Bhuiya-Khan (9)

Stargazing

The stars I see let my wish be free
To the wish, it's allowed to be.
Upon the shooting stars I see,
Let my royalty grow and shine,
Grow and shine like the ancient mine
Which was like a vine doing a mime with a rhyme.
So let this wish be what it's meant to be in the box that I love
And the pieces that my heart can hold.
The box in my heart and my heart in my soul,
Which is in me and that comes to the end,
So if you should share to a friend.

Hope Marshall (9)

Is There A Possibility Of Extraterrestrial Life?

Within realms beyond our sun
Curiosity lingers, is there alien fun?
Imagine a habitable Planet B,
Life would be able to smile with glee.
Could I hold a star?
Would lack of radiation
And oxygen mean a rust-free car?
Strange geological formations and alien flora,
Am I the next Dora Explorer?
Flying cars, aliens all make me ponder,
Would a trip there make me fonder?
Day by day, night by night
We wonder about this quite magnificent sight.

Muazah Mohammed (11)

Waiting

Asleep,
Waiting
Till they can greet the shimmering summer sun
Petals tightly closed...
Sleeping,
Waiting,
Rows upon rows standing guard,
Waiting
Ready to salute
Mist dances through the leaves
Waiting
The early morning rays
Gently touching the velvety petals,
Stretching awake.
Each petal slowly uncurling
Releasing their bright colours to the world.
Turning their heads to look at the sun
Welcoming the new day.

Lorna Sedgwick (9)

The Blizzard

A blizzard of hate blows...
I twisted and turned; I followed you here.
To this land below the clouds,
To this land above the sea.

I carried on, ignoring the chaos and destruction,
I destroyed your joy, your life,
I destroyed this place,
I am the blizzard of snow and wind and ice.

The trees fell,
The land crumbled in the palm of my hand,
Now I will come and seal your fate,
I am the blizzard and for no one I wait...

Tilly Daykin (10)

Fun Times

F amily days are the best ever made,
U p high on trampolines, we jump, race and trade!
N ever a boring day when we're with our mum,

T heme parks, funfairs, parks or softplay, we always have a blast.
I go on the slide while my twin zooms ahead,
M um's always cheering, even when we get red!
E very adventure we have, we laugh and explore,
S uper fun memories we have - and we always want more!

Aidan Ahmat (7)

Busy, Busy Hummingbird

Busy, busy hummingbird buzzing in the trees,
60 wing beats a second,
Is a lot of hard work,
Buzzing round the trees and flowers.

Busy, busy hummingbird buzzing around the flowers,
Never ever a second to stop,
Lots and lots of nectar needed
To buzz around the trees.

Busy, busy hummingbird buzzing back home,
Fly, fly across the sky,
Back to her little nest,
Cosy and comfy she settles down,
As her chicks shuffle around.

Abigail McCullough (10)

Autumn

Can you feel the weather getting colder?
The leaves in the trees growing older
Everyone around
You can see yellow, orange, red
The trees were all filled with green
A colour that can now not be seen
Crunch!
Leaves so dry
All on the ground they lie
There is now so much rain
School starts again
As we enter the building's gate
Animals start to hibernate
It's a long time till June
But it will be winter soon!

Heena Gupta (11)

Stars At Night

Once on a dark, dark night,
I was looking up at the stars,
It looked like the most powerful one was smiling at me.
I thought it was looking down at me,
And I thought it wanted to be friends with me,
But I would never know?

The star was smiling like the happiest star or thing ever to exist.
The star wasn't an ordinary star,
It was a rainbow star!
In my heart, I will always know, that I will have this star as my friend.

Elise Jones (9)

Dreadful Monster

M agnificent
O range claws
N ice
S hort red hair
T alented
E erie voice
R eally small nose

This is a good monster
He has good adjectives
He is nice.

M ischievous
O range claws
N ot very nice
S uch long blue hair
T roublesome
E vil voice
R ed nose

This is a bad monster
He has bad adjectives
He is not nice.

Abdullah Umar (9)

Bookworm

R eading takes you to a different world
E very night, I am captivated by mysterious and treacherous chapters
A dverbs and adjectives paint a vivid scene
D ictionaries help me to understand words I don't recognise
I am transported to forests and foreign lands by the words on the page
N ight by night, the books keep me up past midnight
G oing to sleep is not an option when my favourite book awaits!

Lily-Mae Gladwin (9)

My Favourite Car

A German car with rims so clean,
The callipers shine in the summer sun,
His logo is a big, tall horse,
Rearing on its hind legs,
A rear-wheel-drive car.

The paint is so reflective and glossy, like a mirror,
Two huge exhaust pipes shooting flames out the back,
A 3.8-litre twin-turbo engine as loud as a lion's roar,
Leather seats as comfy as when you get to that bed
after a long day.
It's not what you think it is.

Hunter Crabtree (10)

Island Dream

Sunshine warm and skies so blue,
Palm trees swaying just for you.
Mango juice drips down your chin,
Steel drums play, let the fun begin.

Barefoot runs on sandy shores,
Waves that laugh and ask for more.
Roti, patties and sweet fruit too,
Island life is made for you.

Jamaica, Montserrat and many more,
Sun shining on their shores,
From ocean views to sandy beach,
I'm dreaming of an island dream.

RaVell Noble-Crosbourne (7)

My Own Special Wonderverse

It's full of magical stuff, old and new,
Everything from fiction to true.
They all originate from my dreams,
In their own wonder beams.
Hair, make-up and poems too,
All sorts of things I like to do;

Harry Potter magic,
Animals speaking English,
Rainbows and unicorns,
Elves everywhere,
Every member of my family there too,
Really exciting adventures I go on to do.
In my own special Wonderverse!

Hareer Akram (10)

Whispers Of The Infinite

The sun, the stars,
So bright, they glow.
The small particles
Around them - smoothly flow.

The luminous
Moondust gentle twirls.
Galaxies like Andromeda
Rapidly swirls.

The universe, a boundless sea,
Hums ancient songs in mystery.
Each planet spins, each comet flies,
Like whispers stitched across the skies.

So when the night grows calm and wide,
Let wonder be your only guide...

Ahan Sanu (9)

The Third Time

The third time I ran into a lamppost, I went to the same hospital as before. This time, Social Services were very suspicious of my parents. When questioned, I explained firmly to them that Blindfold Racing, which I hope will soon become an Olympic Sport, was all I'd dreamed about ever since I could walk. They agreed that a Blindfold Baton Pass, although slightly hazardous, sounded like a fun idea and that I wouldn't need a brain scan until next time.

Ava Harris (11)

Darkness

Darkness and death surround me,
As distant as anything could be.
I die ever quicker,
My body becomes thinner.
Screams from above,
Not a single bit of love.
Will I ever get out,
With no one about.
Bones rot,
In the darkest spot.

I hear the shriek of a crow,
I want to go.
You may ask me,
Why am I not free?
I was captured in war, you see,
And now everyone is dead around me.

Josie Smith (8)

Piggiverse!

As my feet leave
The metallic ground of the spaceship
I feel the familiar crunch of leaves on the floor.
I walk forward
Relieved to have left the small, cramped space of the rocket.
Boom!
The ground shakes!
Then comes another one
And another one.
The crashing sounds and
Small, mini earthquakes keep on shaking the floor.
I stop in my tracks.
A colossal guinea pig is racing towards me!

Erin Potter (10)

The Time Machine

Once there was a boy,
Who went to Egypt with joy.
His name was Tim,
And he was very slim.
When he arrived at his destination,
He complained about transportation.
Then he met his uncle,
So asked for his carbuncle.
When his uncle said, "No, it is not for your age,"
He went into a rage.
Then his cousins came,
They both looked the same.
Soon they went to Giza,
And had some pizza.

Ammaar Akram (10)

Grandma's Heart Is An Endless Dream

Grandma's heart is an endless dream
A life, a magic train
Grandma's heart is a ticket to everywhere
A flying aeroplane
Grandma's heart is Pandora's box
A mysterious sea under the waves
Grandma's heart is the key
A secret cave
Grandma's heart is a shooting star
A kind heart to everyone
The Northern Lights
Grandma's heart will always live on inside of us.

Amelie Grace Taylor (9)

Books

My books are filled with stories
They were stacked up on the floor
And when I was bored, I'd pick one up
And read more, more, more.

Nowadays, I've read all of them
One book took me to the shore
Another to the moon
And one even inside a peach's core.

Books are filled with adventures
Just waiting to be seen
So sit and get comfortable
And always be keen.

Arabella Barton (11)

The Piano

A piano makes a wonderful sound,
In a musician's house it's found,
A piano is fun to play,
I wish I could do it all day!

The Wibbly Waltz is my favourite piece to play,
For it's easy as smushing clay,
I can play it again and again,
If it were a competition, judges would give me a ten,

But nothing's as good,
As the piano making a sound,
Except some pud!

Varaa Madhok (8)

Old Flyer

Old Flyer with a belly full of fire,
Belly like a big hot fryer,
Tongue as hard as a tyre,
Always a bore and a trier.

Old Flyer with a belly full of fire,
You thief! You rogue! You liar!
You misfit multiplier!
Always a hider but never a crier.

Old Flyer with a belly full of fire,
Your screech is a terrifier,
As you fly up higher,
In your full dragon attire.

Micah Biddle (9)

The Moon Remembers Me

Amongst the hush of midnight trees,
A howl stirs deep within.
My skin is flesh, but soul runs wild,
The forest knows its long-lost child.

The stars reflect what eyes can't see,
A heartbeat shaped by lupine plea.
Though human hands reach towards the sky,
A tail of thought flicks nearby.

The moon, an old associate, glows solemnly,
In silver light, she remembers me.

Imogen Griffiths (11)

I'm A Nature Nerd

My name is Carson
I'm a nature nerd
Let's go outside
To find a bird
Flying high
Or sat in a tree
Can you hear
The buzzy bee?
Collecting nectar
From a flower
A honey-making
Superpower
You rush around
But nature is slow
Take a moment
Go with the flow
My name is Carson
I love to explore
I belong in the wild wood
For evermore.

Carson-Clae Congreve (6)

Beer And My Dad

For my dad

Beer for my dad is like a cure,
A moment of peace so pure.

Beer is yellow and nice,
Chilled in the fridge not once but twice
Only for Dad to drink.

Dad is white and smart,
Chilling with the beer
Not once but twice.

Dad likes whiskey better,
But Mum doesn't like it.

All my family is good
So is beer!
(This is for joke purposes only.)

Vanya Tkachenko (10)

Night Sky

I look up at the sky,
The sky stares back at me,
There are millions of stars as far as I can see!
I wonder where, I wonder how.
How are the stars just showing up now?
As far as I know, they came long ago,
But as soon as the day breaks, their shine starts to low.
I wonder - how far do the stars go?
Do they go to and fro?
They come and they go,
The pretty night sky, oh my!

Felicity Close (9)

Colours Of Similes

Jam is red as a cherry.
Tangerines are orange as a carrot.
The sun is yellow as a lemon.
The grass is green as pistachio ice cream.
The sky is blue as the sea.
Purple grapes are purple as an orchid.
Butterflies are pink as a blossom tree.
Chocolate is brown as a brownie.
A shadow is black as a black panther.
A stone is grey as ash.
Glacier is white as a snowflake.

Aamina Batool (8)

The Aquanaut

Aquanauts glide
Protectors of the sea
Playing with the creatures
Catch with more than three

Playing in the Caribbean
The Pacific Ocean too
And by the time you realise it's home time
You're stuck to your friends like glue

Then it gets a bit darker
You say goodbye to your mates
Come home to your parents
And see what your dream creates.

Lucy Goldrein (10)

The Chaotic Classroom

Paper planes are everywhere
The teacher's shouting here and there
The class is way too chaotic
The teacher's taking her antibiotics
The pupils are way too loud
I fear I think they're even proud!
The teacher is fed up
I think she's had enough
She yells, "To the principal's office you go!"
Nobody knows what is going to happen tomorrow.

Thomas Prior (10)

Vikings

V ikings thunder, Vikings roar, Vikings hammer,
Vikings ashore.
I f you hear them coming, lock your door!
K eeping calm will not suffice, they will make you pay
the price.
I won't tolerate acts of gore,
N ever surrender, never snore!
G ive them nothing, don't lose determination,
S o pick up your sword to fight for your nation.

Seamus Gerry (8)

Football

F un team sport for all to play
O utside, inside, anywhere you like
O pposing teams can be hard to beat
T actics talk from the manager at half-time
B right kits fill the football pitch
A ttacking the ball from every position
L earning new football skills every time we play
L oving the feeling when the ball goes in the net.

Thomas Woodward (8)

Turning Ten

Once there was a boy called Ken
And he was turning ten.
He had a friend called Ben.
He was so excited that he ate all the cake,
His mum said, "For goodness' sake."
He played with his toys
And he played with his sand.
His dad put up a tent
But it was bent.
They camped in the tent after a fancy meal,
Ken didn't think it was real!

Thomas Taylor-North (9)

The Rockets

I sat there on the edge,
Just sitting there behind the hedge.
I watched the rockets to the sky,
They went so, so high!
I watched them go zoom,
All the way to the moon.
The aliens looked at the machines,
What amazing, cool scenes!
Then I saw the rockets fall,
All the way into my school!
It looked like a lot of bricks,
For all of us to fix!

Amber Allard (8)

Winter

Winter is my favourite time of year...
But summer brings joy and brings a smiling sun
Winter is my favourite time of year...
But autumn brings a luscious brown, a crown of leaves
Winter is my favourite time of year...
But spring brightens up winter's snowy gleam
I look at winter, summer, autumn and spring, knowing just one thing...
They will come again!

Wren Jones (8)

The Poem Of Dust

I am a speck of dust
I am Saturn's rings
On this dangerous journey
I am nothing but everything.

What leads ahead must go on
The path is lit by ice and rock
Travelling through eternity
No race to beat the clock.

There's no time to spare
As time goes at pace
It is a race till it devours you
The black hole of space.

Gene Coleman (9)

Football Mania

Liverpool and Birmingham are playing tonight,
If Birmingham lose, I'll feel alright,
Because I support both teams,
They're always in my dreams,
I go with my friends on the train,
It's crowded, loud and insane,
The game finally ends 2-2,
Liverpool red, Birmingham blue,
I feel happy that it's a draw,
I go home to sleep and snore.

Harry Callinan (8)

The Earth

The Earth was a green paradise,
But now it's grey.
The Earth once was a huge smile
And now it's a frown.
The Earth was kind, but we declined,
Then the Earth realised.
We are on the wrong side of the dice,
We didn't know the Earth got worse.
More and more the Earth got rotten,
But then we realised
The Earth needs help.

Adam Aboumandil (8)

Ancient Egypt

E gypt, a country of mystery, pyramids and mighty kings
G ods and goddesses represented natural forces of things
Y ellow sands known as the Great Sand Sea
P haraohs called Cleopatra, Tutankhamun and Rameses
T he hieroglyphics, a language built up of objects, actions, sounds and ideas. Treasures and curses lost over the years.

Everlyn Baker (9)

My Family Is The Best

My family is my best friend,
My mum's cooking is 10/10.

My dad works very hard,
So I can spend money on his credit card.

My little sister loves lollipops,
I think she's a cheeky chops.

My brother puts me to shame,
When he loses on his video game.

My family is great,
We're all best mates.

Jonah Petty (7)

The Fabulous, Flaming Phoenix

In a mountain oh so high,
Right up in the sky,
Is a cave of stormy stone,
No one has ever known,
Soaring in is a bird of fire,
A phoenix this is, to my desire,
Twisting and turning like a ballerina,
It fizzled and popped like Orangina,
From the tips of my hair to the tips of my toes,
Inside of me, a feeling of awe arose.

Bethan Johnson (10)

Spring

When the sun is no longer shy
The birds in my garden fly high
The colourful flowers grow
And neighbours are starting to say 'hello!'

The goslings are out, learning to swim
They duck and they dive, on the water they skim
Some people are sneezing from the pollen that flies
But I run and I play, saying winter goodbyes.

India Arnby-Lumley (7)

A Teddy Bear's Party

T ime to party
E ager to rave
D ancing through darkness
D aylight has disappeared
Y ummy treats

B ears coming to celebrate
E xquisite buffet
A ll night, we have fun
R elaxing all day
S weets being scoffed

That's a teddy bear's party.

Alice Evans (10)

Whispers

M ythical forest beyond your eyes.
Y elling for you to come inside.
T he mythical animals swing on the treetops with
H ealing bananas and jumping elephants.
I n the deep there rests a magical cave
C ooling back
A nd rough skin
L ies a mysterious dragon which is as heavy as a
wagon.

Favour Oladepo (8)

London

North, South, East and West,
My love for London never ends.
Each curve and turn,
In every street,
Happy emotions always meet.

It might be old,
It might be cold,
But amazing are many places.
There's Ilford Lane and Central,
Green Street, oh and Southall.

But the best of all,
Was my own home.

Hafsa Umar (8)

A Day Of Fun

The kitten chased a butterfly,
Dancing through the morning sky.
The puppy chewed his owner's shoe,
Luckily, it wasn't new.
The puppy rested in his bed,
He settled down his sleepy head.
The kitten curled up in the sun,
Tired from a day of fun.
They slept right through the darkest night,
To play again in morning's light.

Eve Newcombe (8)

All About Fairies

Fairies are kind,
Fairies are mild,
And they can be so wild,
Fairies can do magic,
Fairies' favourite animal is a snake,
Fairies love eating cake,
They share it by a shining lake,
Fairies can turn the dark into light,
Fairies can turn day into night,
Fairies' favourite plants are flowers,
If you see them, then you have powers.

Judy Mohammed (8)

Swim, Swim, Swim

The pressure is on, the crowd is wild
On every block, there stands a child
In position ready to dive,
Having waited months for this moment to arrive.

They hear the start and off they glide
Into the water, side by side,
Arms like windmills, swim, swim, swim!
Who will be the fastest and win, win, win!

Evelyn Foster (9)

Wonder Poem

All around me are lovely flowers in the room
Filled with sparkle and spooky gloom
The vibrant place is full of marvellous nature
This is a wonderful, excited adventure
I could feel the shiny clouds
Whizzing and zooming just as loud
Surrounding me was a stunning gleam
It was like a magical dream.

Jiya Sahota (8)

Hidden Danger

I see some stars in the sky, high above
Although it looks pretty
Danger lurks everywhere
The zombies..
Yes... the zombies are bound to appear from the ground
They live in the dark
Some of their skin is the colour of bark
So make that leap over a huge crack
Leave and don't look back.

Minuli Uduwela (9)

The Land

As I woke up, a fresh breeze hit me,
Clouding the fears of dangers in my mind.
As the birds chirped, the branches waved,
Like they were keeping time.

A soft, furry horse galloped across
The beautiful, unbarren-like land.
Her brown fur gleamed with dazzling smiles
Of what she lived, a bunch of denial.

Yethum Athukorala (9)

Dragons

D readful dragons breathing fire,
R uby red and glorious green,
A scending up and soaring higher,
G nashing bones until they're clean,
O bsessive over meat,
N othing better, what a treat,
S pecial and mythical, that is what dragons are.

Ruby Cohen (9)

Who Am I?

Who am I?
I have huge wings to fly
And I fly high in the sky
I'm a mythical creature
With a fiery feature
I'm covered in a hot amber flame
And not all my species are the same
Oh, and my name rhymes with Kleenex
Can't you guess, no?
I'm a phoenix!

Grace Donington (9)

Henry VIII

H orrible
E vil
N asty
R otund
Y oung (not very!)

T ough
H ungry
E gocentric

V ery demanding
I ngenious
I mpossible to please
I nsatiable appetite for beheadings.

Annie Collins (9)

The Perfect Sight

The moon is bright.
The moon is huge.
It is the only moon in the darkening night.
The sun is hot.
The sun is bright.
It is the only sun in the shining light.
I love the moon, but light is something else.
Dark is the opposite of light.
Which is your perfect sight?

April Postill (8)

Spring

S ap as sticky as glue
E ggshells as white as the clouds
A pples as red as ketchup
S wans as aggressive as an angry dragon
O xeye daisies as delicate as ants
N ature as lively as dogs
S wallowtails as colourful as a rainbow.

William Stannett (10)

Jerry's World

Come with me to a world of pure imagination.
When I went to the Jurassic Park exhibition, there were dinosaurs,
Big and small, friendly and tall, green and yellow,
And even brown.
I saw it all.
Open your eyes,
You can see it,
To believe in your imagination.

Jerry Connors (9)

The Swimming Race

On the block.
Heart beating.
Take your mark.
Beep.
Dive in.
Kicking hard.
Faster,
Faster.
Arms aching.
Tumble turn.
Streamline underwater.
Lungs bursting.
Breath.
Kick.
Finish.
First place.
Gold medal.

Beata Kalthi (11)

Powerful Phoenix

P owerful as an angry elephant
H as immortality like a god
O btains renewal and new life
E xcellent flying abilities
N umerous, invincible, fiery feathers
I nferno breaks, then builds again
X marks the spark of life.

Seen Leung (10)

Majestic Dragons

D ragons could fly in the sky.
R ampaging dragons are mighty.
A s powerful lightning, it could breathe colourful fire.
G reen body for camouflaging in the wilderness.
O range eyes for destruction.
N oxious dragons are deadly.

Mathiyazhagan Manikandan (10)

The Robin

Robin on the branch,
Sings a song of 'Where are you?'
Her voice stays quiet.
Small wings fluttering,
Huddled in the morning sun,
She longs for warm hugs.
Bright eyes, searching skies,
Collecting glimmers of you,
One for sorrow, two...

Alice Young (9)

Summer

Summer, a gift from the world,
Summer, come stay for a while.

S tay hot out of the sun
U nder a fun shade
M ake yourself a smoothie
M ake yourself laugh
E nter summer
R un around while enjoying summer.

Aliza Shahid (10)

African Fish Eagle

Eagle flying oh so high
Ruler of the big, blue sky
High above the African plain
Inkwazi is your Zulu name.

Sitting high up in your tree
Looking at what you can see
You spread your wings and with a swish
You catch a shiny fish.

Michael Annett (8)

The Leprechaun

Haiku poetry

Peace in the forest,
A tranquil, quiet clearing,
No one to be seen.

A noise in the bush,
A silhouette in the grass,
Nothing to be seen,

A high-pitched giggle,
Could it be you, Leprechaun?
A leaf-green flash - yes.

Erin Glynn-Colyer (11)

Orchestra Of The Environment

Did you know? The world can sing, you just need to listen!
The sun shines bright like a stage light, bright and beautiful.
As the wind whistles the chorus, leaves dance to the tune that the bushes rustle.
So try to listen to the song of the world.

Harriet Beech (10)

My Dog, Lucky

My dog likes sticks,
She also likes to lick,
She snores like a pig,
But she is not big,
She is fast,
But sometimes comes last,
She is not tall,
But she loves to play ball,
She is the colour tan,
And I am her fan.

Reggie Gibson (8)

The Great War

A clashing of titans
A battle of giants
An army of warriors
The conflict of rivals
The bloodshed of many
The struggle for power
The dispute of the century
The rivalry of monarchs
The war has only begun.

Anya Vidanage (11)

Flowers

F lowers
L ooks like happiness
O pens like a banana peeling
W ardens open up in our mind
E very day flowers bloom like joy
R oots standing
S trange like a baby tree.

Samantha Hull (9)

Friendship

F un
R are
I nspirational
E verlasting
N ice
D elightful
S upportive
H appy
I nseparable
P atient

It's my friends.

Matthew Townsend (8)

Over The Rainbow

R ed and orange
A bit of green
I love the rainbow
N ever coloured black
B lue skies after rain
O h, rainbow over the clouds
W hite clouds like cotton candy.

Lexi Watkins (9)

Unicorns

U nicorns are beautiful
N ice shiny manes
I love unicorns
C olourful tales
O range mane
R osy cheeks
N ice, sparkly gold horn
S oft fur.

Elin Hughes (7)

The Life In Me

We all wear masks
But it doesn't matter to me.

When midnight strikes
I climb out of bed
And howl to the moon

The world is wild.
My heart is free
And the life in me.

Celia Elizabeth Cryne (11)

The Poor Tree

Twisted by the wind
It's curling like a hand
It's a poor tree
It's grown on the hill
With so many words
And so many thoughts
Darkness covers the tree
But never broke it.

Tyler James Crawford (9)

Dragons

D eadly and dramatic
R ampant and ravenous
A ggressive and ardent
G rand and golden
O utrageous and overconfident
N asty and nonstop.

Dragons!

Quintin Kleiser (8)

My Dragon

M orning sleeper
Y awn fire

D reamer steamer
R oarer drawer
A mazing flyer
G ood friend
O ver sleeper
N ight mornings.

Emilia Menezes-Shotter (9)

Birthdays

The excitement was building,
The door was opened,
People were heard,
Hellos were said,
Sweets were given,
Happy birthday was sung,
The birthday was over
But another to come!

Milly Hirst (9)

Nature

Down on Earth where dirt lies,
I tiptoe through the forest.
Do you hear the birds chirping
Or foxes snoring away.
I spot some squirrels racing up the tree
And now I see you and me.

Freya Hartfield (8)

Smiling Man

Creepy smile,
Long legs,
Fast run,
Brings horror,
Sharp teeth,
Likes screens,
Old clothes,
Ball shadow,
Leaves dark,
Cold body,
Red eyes,
Loud steps.

Karl Anderson (9)

It's Finally Autumn

Rain falls
Umbrellas go up
Coats on
Sunglasses off
Leaves crackle
Wellies squelch
Birds migrate
Hedgehogs hibernate
Loud fireworks
Quiet people staring.

Violet Johns (9)

The Flowers

The flowers grow when you're happy.
The flowers go down when you're sad.
The flowers grow big when you're angry
But you always have a flower
When you have feelings.

Erin Harrison (10)

Dragon

D ragon is dreadful
R ed with flames
A nyone who comes close burns with fear
G rrr does the dragon
O ut goes his fire
N ame is Fury.

Cerys Hughes (8)

Stars

S tars are magic
T rophies in the sky
A mazing space rockets fly by
R adiant sun shines bright
S parkling stars in the night.

Juliette Murray-Atkinson (5)

Porcus

P iggies fly
O riginal and grateful
R eally crazy
C ute and gorgeous
U nbelievable magical hooves
S uper as ever.

Astarla Bishop (12)

Wizards

Magicat, mystical
Brewing, cursing, enchanting,
Warlocks, witches, gremlins, goblins
Mystifying, riddling, bamboozling,
Secretive, curious
Magic!

Sebastien Body (11)

Valentina

Blossom child
Orchard of youth
First apple
Arrived like a flaming sword

Gentle ocean
Unfold
With first love
First verdict
Life not bitter
Life changed
First from
Eden.

Milagros Bryce (10)

Unicorns

Unicorns
Magical, beautiful
Galloping, watching, glittering
Mane, legs, eyes, tail
Waiting, shining, shimmering
Elegant, silky
Unicorns.

Adhithi Vinoth (7)

Wizards Of Stafford

The wizards of Stafford are hidden in plain sight,
Their magic wristbands are very tight.
They only show themselves at night,
Fighting dragons in their spare time.

Charlie Kemp (10)

Imagination

Let your spirit fly,
Float into the sky,
Let your imagination burst,
Let it be first,
Welcome in the creative.

Lyla Johnson (9)

Pirates

A man as scary as a ghost.
They eat things like beans and toast.
They are on the ship with highs and lows.

Spencer Everett (8)

Space

S uper
P robably
A mazing
C atastrophe
E mpathetic.

Ismail Qureshi (7)

Bunnies Hopping

A haiku

Bunnies hopping round
On the fresh, crumbly brown mound
Of smelly, wet ground.

Inés Fortunat Gill

Half-Term

A haiku

It's nearly half-term
Time to say goodbye to school
But we will be back

Poppy Eccles (9)

A Seaside Summer

A haiku

Salty sea breezes,
Tiny freckles on my nose,
Golden hour sunsets.

Isabella Welborn (10)

YOUNG WRITERS INFORMATION

We hope you have enjoyed reading this book – and that you will continue to in the coming years.

If you're the parent or family member of an enthusiastic poet or story writer, do visit our website **www.youngwriters.co.uk/subscribe** and sign up to receive news, competitions, writing challenges and tips, activities and much, much more! There's lots to keep budding writers motivated!

If you would like to order further copies of this book, or any of our other titles, then please give us a call or order via your online account.

Young Writers
Remus House
Coltsfoot Drive
Peterborough
PE2 9BF
(01733) 890066
info@youngwriters.co.uk

Join in the conversation!
Tips, news, giveaways and much more!

YoungWritersUK **YoungWritersCW**
youngwriterscw **youngwriterscw**

Scan to watch the video!